The Future of Home Schooling

Author of:

Anonymous Tip [novel] 1996

How a Man Prepares His Daughters for Life 1996

The Homeschooling Father 1993

Where Do I Draw the Line? 1992

Constitutional Law for Christian Students 1991

Home Schooling and the Law 1990

The
Future of
Home
Schooling

A New Direction for
Christian Home Education

Michael Farris

REGNERY PUBLISHING, INC.
Washington, D.C.

Library of Congress Cataloging-in-Publication Data

Farris, Michael P., 1951-
    The Future of Home Schooling: a new direction for Christian home education / Michael Farris.
       p.   cm.
    Includes bibliographical references and index.
    ISBN 0-89526-700-4 (alk. paper)
    1. Home schooling—United States. 2. Christian education—United States. I. Title.
    LC40.F37 1997
    371.04'2—dc21   97-15529
                                                CIP

Published in the United States by
Regnery Publishing, Inc.
An Eagle Publishing Company
422 First Street, SE
Washington, DC 20003

Distributed to the trade by
National Book Network
4720-A Boston Way
Lanham, MD 20706

Printed on acid-free paper
Manufactured in the United States of America

10 9 8 7 6 5 4 3 2 1

Books are available in quantity for promotional or premium use. Write to Director of Special Sales, Regnery Publishing, Inc., 422 First Street, SE, Suite 300, Washington, DC 20003, for information on discounts and terms or call (202) 546-5005.

To Jim Carden, my late friend who gave HSLDA and home schooling a brighter future by his enthusiastic support.

Contents

Overview of the Home Schooling Phenomenon

H ome schooling is a flourishing phenomenon within the United States. In the early 1980s, the general public had never heard of home schooling, but today, almost everyone has.

Still, society at large knows little about home schoolers: their backgrounds, their activities, or their achievements. A recent study conducted by Dr. Brian Ray, president of the National Home Education Research Institute (NHERI), provides some answers.

This study, *Strengths of Their Own: Home Schoolers Across America*, collected data on 5,402 home school students from 1,657 families for the 1994–95 and 1995–96 academic years. Nearly 6,000 surveys were sent to home school families using a variety of sources and methods. Some were mailed directly to families (both those randomly selected from numerous mailing lists as well as longitudinal participants from Ray's similar study

This overview is a reprint of *Home Education Across the United States*, reprint permission granted by Brian Ray and Home School Legal Defense Association. The full study can be obtained by contacting National Home Education Research Institute (NHERI) at P.O. Box 13939; 925 Cottage Street N.E.; Salem, OR 97309; (503) 364-1490.

How Many Home Schoolers Are There?

Figure 1.0 – Home School Students Nationwide
Compared to Selected State Public School Populations

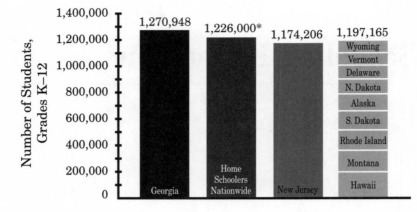

* This study calculated that there were 1.23 million home school students in the U.S. during the fall of 1996. The estimated margin of error for this calculation is ± 10%, yielding a range of 1,103,000 to 1,348,000. This is similar to the total public school enrollment of Georgia or New Jersey (ranked 9th and 10th largest respectively among state public school populations nationwide).

Public school state enrollment figures are for 1994 and the most recent available, based on a table from the U.S. Department of Education, Office of Educational Research & Improvement, National Center for Education Statistics (1996, November); Digest of Education Statistics (1996); Washington, DC: U.S. Department of Education.

---

in 1990). Others were blindly forwarded to families through the leadership of independent home school support groups and networks operating in every state. Unquestionably, this research represents the largest and most comprehensive study on home schooling ever undertaken.*

In a collaborative effort to provide solid answers to common questions about home schooling, HSLDA and Dr. Ray have highlighted some of the key findings of this study. Where available, comparable public school student data were also obtained.

---

* Brian D. Ray, *Strengths of Their Own—Home Schoolers Across America: Academic Achievement, Family Characteristics, and Longitudinal Traits*, 1997, Salem, OR: National Home Education Research Institute.

How Do Home School Students Score?

Figure 2.0

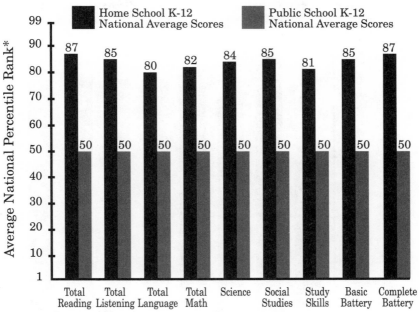

Achievement Test Subject Areas

Data collected for standardized academic achievement tests for the 1994–95 academic year.

* For more detail about the non-equal-interval nature of a simple percentile scale which has distortion especially near the ends of the scale see Ray (1997).

Just how prevalent is home education today? The data indicate there are approximately 1.23 million American children being taught at home. This finding (which has an estimated margin of error of ±10%) exceeds the total public school enrollment for the state of New Jersey, which has the tenth largest student population in the nation. Put another way, there are more home school students nationwide than there are public school students in Wyoming, Vermont, Delaware, North Dakota, Alaska, South Dakota, Rhode Island, Montana, and Hawaii—*combined*. In fact, America's home schoolers collectively outnumber the individual statewide public school enrollments in each of forty-one states (Figure 1.0).

How Do Long-Term Home Schoolers Compare to Those Who Switch to Home Education Midstream?

Figure 3.0—Achievement for Eighth Grade Home Schoolers Segmented by Years Taught at Home

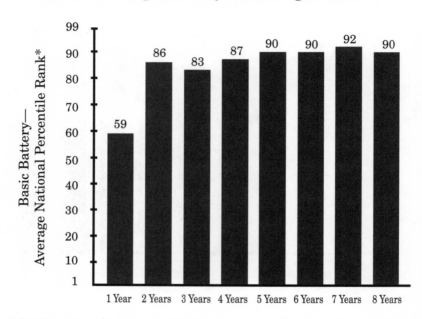

* See Ray (1997) for more detail about the non-equal-interval nature of a simple percentile scale which has distortion especially near the ends of the scale.

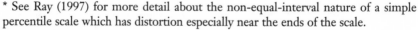

Why are so many parents choosing to home school? Because it works. This study shows that home educated students excel on nationally-normed standardized achievement exams. On average, home schoolers out-perform their public school peers by 30 to 37 percentile points across all subjects (Figure 2.0).

In fact, home schoolers' test scores sometimes increase in relation to the number of years a student has been taught at home. The data for eighth grade home schoolers suggest that those who have completed two or more years at home score substantially higher than those who just completed one year of instruction (Figure 3.0). This suggests that students who move from an institutional school to home school may experience a brief transition period. Students home schooled

Is Teacher Certification Necessary
for High Achievement?

Figure 4.0

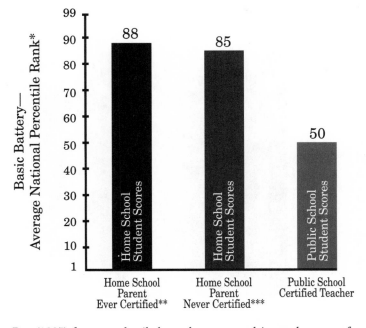

* See Ray (1997) for more detail about the non-equal-interval nature of a simple percentile scale which has distortion especially near the ends of the scale.
    ** Either parent ever certified.
    *** Neither parent ever certified.
    Home school data are for grades K–12.

from early grades tend to score higher in subsequent years in some subject areas (see Ray, 1997).

Critics often claim that only parents with teaching credentials can effectively home school. The data from this study suggest otherwise. Home school students' test scores segmented by whether their parents have ever held a teaching certificate reveal a differential of only three percentile points—the 88th percentile versus the 85th percentile (Figure 4.0).

Futhermore, a parent's education background has no substantive

Does Parent Education Level
Predict Student Achievement?

For Home Schoolers: NO!

Figure 5.1—Home School Achievement—Basic Battery Test

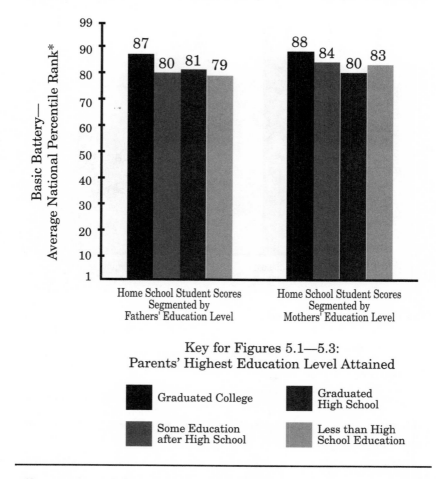

Key for Figures 5.1—5.3:
Parents' Highest Education Level Attained

█ Graduated College   █ Graduated High School

█ Some Education after High School   █ Less than High School Education

---

effect on their children's home school academic performance, according to this study. Home educated students' test scores remain between the 80th and 90th percentiles, whether their mothers have a college degree or did not complete high school (Figure 5.1).

For public school students, however, a parent's education level *does* affect their children's performance (Figures 5.2 & 5.3). In eighth grade

Does Parent Education Level Predict Student Achievement?

For Public Schoolers: YES!

Figure 5.2—Public School Achievement—Writing Test**   **Figure 5.3—Public School Achievement—Math Test****

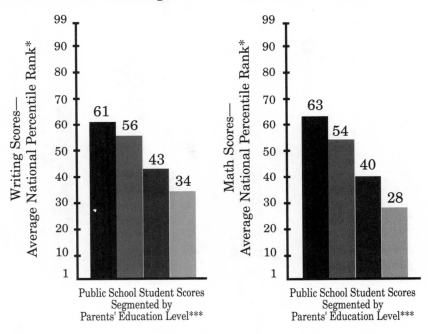

Public School Student Scores Segmented by Parents' Education Level***   Public School Student Scores Segmented by Parents' Education Level***

* See Ray (1997) for more detail about the non-equal-interval nature of a simple percentile scale which has distortion especially near the ends of the scale.

** Basic battery achievement test scores not available for public school students.

*** Public school data are for eighth grade writing scores and thirteen-year-olds' math scores based on tables from the U.S. Department of Education, Office of Educational Research & Improvement, National Center for Education Statistics (1996, November); National Assessment of Educational Progress (NAEP) trends in academic progress [trends report and appendices]; Washington, DC: U.S. Department of Education.

Home school data are for grades K–12.

---

math, public school students whose parents are college graduates score at the 63rd percentile, whereas students whose parents have less than a high school diploma score at the 28th percentile. Remarkably, students taught at home by mothers who never finished high school

How Do Minorities Fare in Home Education?

Figure 6.1—Race Relationship to Reading Test Scores

Figure 6.2—Race Relationship to Mathematics Test Scores

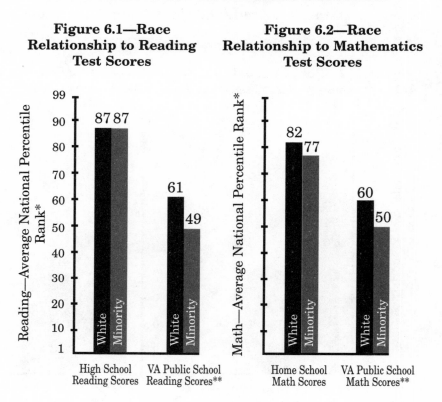

* See Ray (1997) for more detail about the non-equal-interval nature of a simple percentile scale which has distortion especially near the ends of the scale.

**Public school achievement data are based on eighth grade scores from Table 4 of The Virginia Assessment Program: Results for the 1995–1996 School Year (1996, July). Richmond, VA: Virginia Department of Education.

The Virginia minority scores were weighted according to the proportions of minorities in this study of home schoolers to arrive at the numbers in this figure. The minority groups were American Indian/Alaskan Native, Asian/Pacific Islander, black, and Hispanic. Of home school minority students tested in this study, about 63% were black or Hispanic.

Public school achievement data are similar for the U.S. in general but the same detail of data was not available for all public schools. See U.S. Department of Education, Office of Educational Research & Improvement, National Center for Education Statistics (1996, November); National Assessment of Educational Progress (NAEP) trends in academic progress [trends report and appendices]; Washington, DC: U.S. Department of Education.

Home school data are for grades K–12.

What About the Gender Gap in Academics?

Figure 7.0

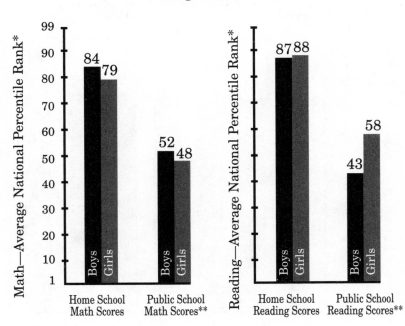

* See Ray (1997) for more detail about the non-equal-interval nature of a simple percentile scale which has distortion especially near the ends of the scale.

** Public school achievement data are for eighth grade based on tables from the U.S. Department of Education, Office of Educational Research & Improvement, National Center for Education Statistics (1996, November); National Assessment of Educational Progress (NAEP) trends in academic progress [trends report and appendices]; Washington, DC: U.S. Department of Education.

Home school data are for grades K–12.

score a full 55 percentile points higher than public school students from families of comparable educational backgrounds.

Does race make a difference in academic performance? Math and reading scores for minority home schoolers show no significant difference when compared to whites. In reading, both white and minority home schoolers score at the 87th percentile. Only five points separate them in math—the 82nd percentile versus the 77th percentile (Figures 6.1 & 6.2).

Is Family Income a Predictor of Academic Achievement for Home Schoolers?

Figure 8.0—No Impact on Achievement

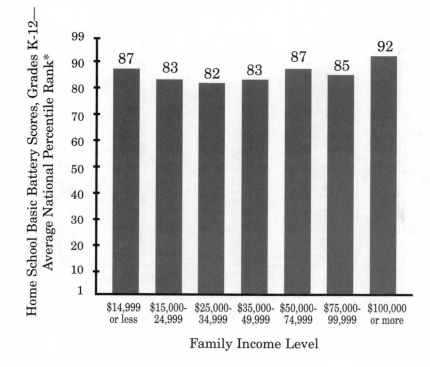

* See Ray (1997) for more detail about the non-equal-interval nature of a simple percentile scale which has distortion especially near the ends of the scale.

A similar comparison for public school students, however, demonstrates a substantial disparity. White public school eighth grade students score at the 57th percentile in reading and at the 58th percentile in math nationally.[1] Black public school eighth grade students score at the 28th percentile in reading and the 24th percentile in math

---

[1] Public school achievement data are for eighth grade based on tables from the U.S. Department of Education, Office of Educational Research & Improvement, National Center for Education Statistics (1996, November). *National Assessment of Educational Progress (NAEP) trends in academic progress* [trends report and appendices]. Washington, DC: U.S. Department of Education.

Does Spending Correlate with Achievement?

Figure 9.0

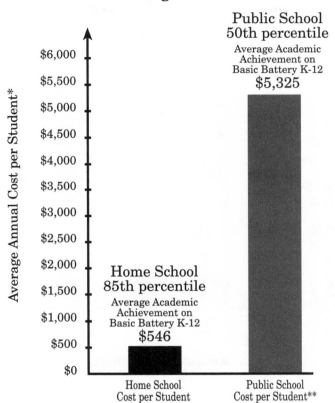

* All cost-per-student amounts in this figure exclude capital costs.

** United States Department of Education, National Center for Education Statistics (1996). Statistics in brief, June 1996; Revenues and expenditures for public elementary and secondary education: School year 1993–1994. [From: Common core of data: National public education financial survey.] Washington, DC: U.S. Department of Education.

in the same national sample. Hispanic students score at the 28th percentile in reading and at the 29th percentile in math nationally. However, national figures are not available which allow proportional weighting of various minority groups to match the same proportions as are found among home schooling racial minority groups.

Is Government Regulation Necessary for
High Achievement?

Figure 10.1—State Regulation:
No Impact on Home School Achievement

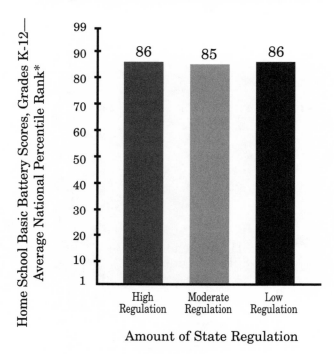

Amount of State Regulation

---

* See Ray (1997) for more detail about the non-equal-interval nature of a simple percentile scale which has distortion especially near the ends of the scale.

Scores are available from the Virginia Department of Public Education, which allows the scores to be weighted in a manner which matches the proportions exactly in the same ratio as are found in the home schooling sample. When the scores are weighted in this fashion, Virginia white eighth grade students score at the 61st percentile in reading while the weighted minorities score at the 49th percentile. In math the same scores show whites at the 60th percentile and minorities at the 50th percentile.

Home schoolers have been able to substantially eliminate the disparity between white and minority scores even when the samples are

Figure 10.2—Breakdown of States by Regulatory Policy

Key for Figure 10.2

 Low Regulation:
No state requirement for parents to initiate any contact with the state.

 High Regulation:
State requires parents to send notification or achievement test scores and/or professional evaluation, plus other requirements (e.g. curriculum approval by the state, teacher qualifications of parents, or home visits by state officials).

Moderate Regulation:
State requires parents to send notification, test scores, and/or professional evaluation of student progress.

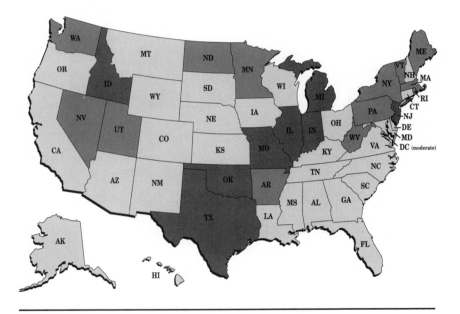

adjusted to reflect the exact same proportion of American Indians, Asians, blacks, and Hispanics.

When segmented by gender, test scores for home schoolers reveal that boys are slightly better in math (the 84th percentile versus the 79th percentile), and girls are somewhat better in reading (the 88th percentile versus the 87th percentile). Public school student performance in math follows a similar pattern, but public school boys'

Do Test Scores Vary by Who Adminstered the Test?

Figure 11.0

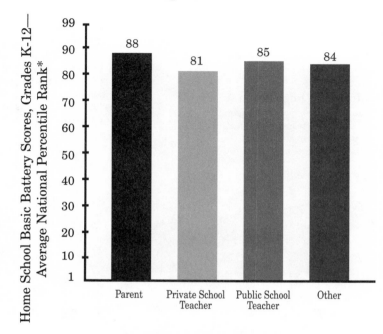

Test Administrator Category

* See Ray (1997) for more detail about the non-equal-interval nature of a simple percentile scale which has distortion especially near the ends of the scale.

reading scores are markedly behind girls', the 43rd percentile versus the 58th percentile—a 15 point difference (Figure 7.0).

Segmenting student test scores by family income shows that socioeconomic status is not a determinant of academic performance for home schoolers (Figure 8.0). Regardless of family income bracket, home school students score between the 82nd and 92nd percentiles.

According to some researchers and officials, family income does have a significant impact on public school students' test scores. Concerned about a recent study of student achievement in the Denver public schools, a school board member wrote, "The conclusion is

How Many Times Do Home Schoolers Visit the Library Per Month?

Figure 12.0

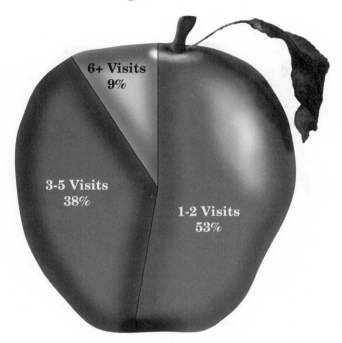

6+ Visits
9%

3-5 Visits
38%

1-2 Visits
53%

Data are for K–12 home school students.

clear. Family income and class are stronger indicators of educational success than race."[2]

A cost-benefit analysis reveals that an average of $546 spent per home school student per year yields an average 85th percentile ranking on test scores. Compare this to the average annual expenditure of $5,325 per public school student to achieve only an average

[2] *Denver Business Journal*, February 21, 1997, p. 40A. See also, Coleman, James S., Thomas Hoffer, & Sally Kilgore, (1982) *High school achievement: Public, Catholic, and private schools compared*, New York, NY: Basic Books. and Snow, Catherine E., Wendy S. Barnes, Jean Chandler, Irene F. Goodman, & Lowry Hemphill, (1991) *Unfulfilled expectations: Home and school influences on literacy*, Cambridge, MA: Harvard University Press.

Are Computers a Part of Home Schools?

Figure 13.0

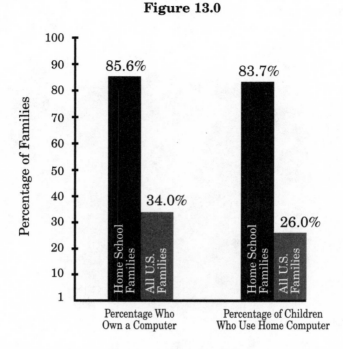

* Data for all U.S. families based on table from United States Department of Education, National Center for Education Statistics. (1996). Digest of education statistics 1996, Table 417: Access to and use of home computers, by selected characteristics of students and other users: October 1993. Washington, DC: U. S. Department of Education.

50th percentile ranking. These figures do not include capital expenditures, like buildings and land, etc. (Figure 9.0).

The degree of governmental regulation from state to state has no significant effect on the academic performance of home schoolers. Whether a state imposes a high degree of regulation (i.e., notification, standardized testing, professional evaluations, curriculum approval, teacher qualifications, home visits, etc.) or no regulation, home school student test score averages are identical—the 86th percentile for both segments (Figure 10.1). Legitimate questions may be asked concerning the purpose of such regulations since there is no apparent effect on student learning.

What About Socialization?

Figure 14.0—Home Schoolers' Activities and Community Involvement

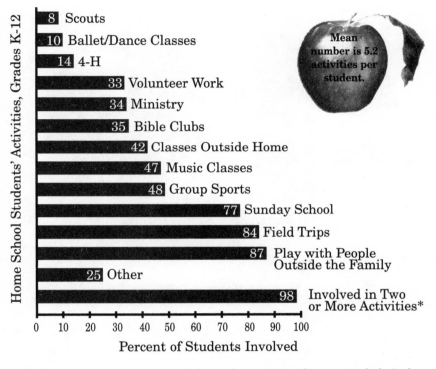

Home School Students' Activities, Grades K-12

Percent of Students Involved

8	Scouts
10	Ballet/Dance Classes
14	4-H
33	Volunteer Work
34	Ministry
35	Bible Clubs
42	Classes Outside Home
47	Music Classes
48	Group Sports
77	Sunday School
84	Field Trips
87	Play with People Outside the Family
25	Other
98	Involved in Two or More Activities*

Mean number is 5.2 activities per student.

* Participation in two or more of the twelve activities does not include "other activities." See Table 8 of Ray (1997).

Standardized tests for home schoolers are administered in various ways. Little difference was found in scores among students tested by a parent, a private school teacher, a public school teacher, or some other test administrator. The average scores range between the 81st and 88th percentiles (Figure 11.0).

What kind of curriculum do home schoolers use? The vast majority of home school parents (71.1%) hand-pick their instructional materials, custom designing the curriculum to presumably suit the needs of their children, their family's lifestyle, and applicable government regulations.

How Many Hours Per Day Are Spent Watching Television and Video Tapes?

Figure 15.0

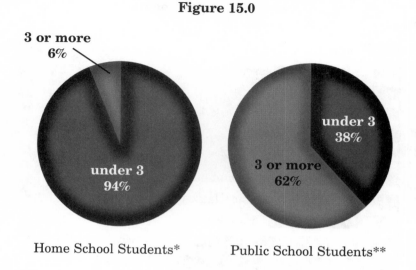

Home School Students*   Public School Students**

* Data reported for K–12 home school students' weekday viewing.

** Data reported for thirteen-year-olds are fairly representative of nine-, thirteen-, and seventeen-year-olds, based on tables from the U.S. Department of Education, Office of Educational Research & Improvement, National Center for Education Statistics (1996, November); National Assessment of Educational Progress (NAEP) trends in academic progress [trends report and appendices]; Washington, DC: U.S. Department of Education.

Nearly 24% use a complete curriculum package purchased from one of numerous providers. Other options include enrollment in private satellite schools or special programs operated by the local private school. The data also revealed that some parents employ more than one approach to assembling their children's curriculum (Table 1.0, page xxvii).

This study found that home schoolers (53%) visit a library at least once or twice each month (Figure 12.0). Nearly half (47%) reported that they go even more often. As a group, home schooled students frequent the library an average of 3.8 times each month (see Ray, 1997).

Apparently quick to employ the cutting-edge technology of personal computers, 85.6% of home school families reported owning a computer and 83.7% say their children use it in their education.

Ages of Home School Students in Study

Figure 16.0

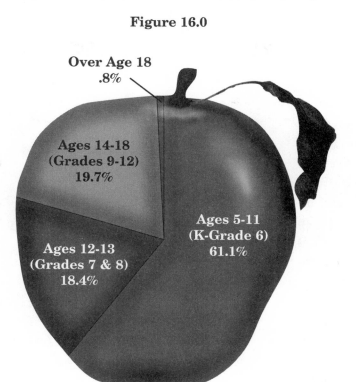

Over Age 18
.8%

Ages 14-18
(Grades 9-12)
19.7%

Ages 12-13
(Grades 7 & 8)
18.4%

Ages 5-11
(K-Grade 6)
61.1%

What Kind of Curriculum Do Home Schoolers Use?

Table 1.0

Type of Curriculum	Usage*
Parent Designed (major components are hand picked)	71.1%
Complete Curriculum Package	23.8%
Satellite School (as source)	3.0%
Home School Program from Local Private School	0.7%
Other	6.5%

* Some parents marked more than one category, so total exceeds 100%.

What Are the Occupations of Home School Parents?

Table 2.0

Occupation	Father	Mother
Farmer, Farm Manager	3.4 %	0.2 %
Homemaker, Home Education	0.5 %	87.7 %
Laborer	2.4 %	0.1 %
Manager	8.9 %	0.3 %
Military	4.3 %	0.1 %
Office Worker	1.1 %	0.8 %
Operator of Machines	3.7 %	0.1 %
Small Business Owner	10.7 %	2.1 %
Professional 1 (Accountant, RN, Engineer, etc.)	17.3 %	4.8 %
Professional 2 (Doctor, Professor, Lawyer, etc.)	16.9 %	1.1 %
Protective Service	1.7 %	0.0 %
Sales	4.3 %	0.1 %
School Teacher	2.2 %	0.9 %
Service Worker	1.0 %	0.4 %
Technical	8.1 %	0.1 %
Tradesperson	6.9 %	0.3 %
Other	6.5 %	0.9 %

Compared to the national norms for all U.S. families (34% and 26%, respectively), home school families are setting a trend for equipping their children with resources for the 21st century (Figure 13.0).

Home schoolers are often asked, "What about socialization?" The data on home school students' activities and community involvement reveal that, on average, these children are engaged in 5.2 activities outside the home, with 98% involved in two or more. Activities ranging from scouts, dance class, and 4-H to sports, field trips, and volunteer work demonstrate that home schoolers interact with people of all ages, from all sorts of backgrounds, and in all types of social settings (Figure 14.0).

This study also measured the time home schoolers spent watching

How Long Are They Going to Home School?

Figure 17.0—Parents' Intent to Continue Home Education

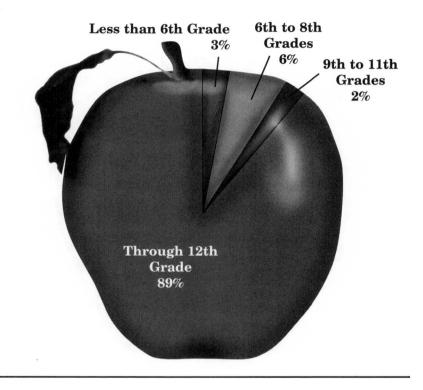

Less than 6th Grade 3%

6th to 8th Grades 6%

9th to 11th Grades 2%

Through 12th Grade 89%

---

television and video tapes each weekday. These data were compared to those for public school students. Simply put, home school children spend substantially less time watching TV than do public school children (Figure 15.0).

Of the 5,402 children included in this study, all grades (K–12) are substantively represented. The majority of the sample (61.1%) is comprised of grades K–6, probably because the movement is relatively young and has grown so rapidly (Figure 16.0).

According to the data, home school parents are employed in a full range of typical occupations. Most notable, however, is the finding that 87.7% of mothers and 0.5% of fathers have elected to stay home full-time to teach and raise their children (Table 2.0).

How Many Years Were Home School Graduates Taught at Home?

Figure 18.0

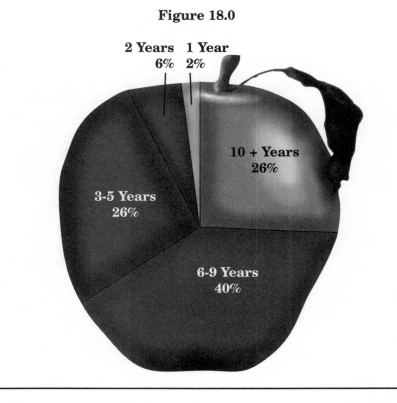

How enthusiastic are home school parents about their success? The vast majority (89%) intend to continue teaching their children at home all the way through high school (Figure 17.0).

On average, home school graduates had 6.9 years of home education (see Ray, 1997). The data reveal that 92% of graduates were taught at home for three or more years (Figure 18.0).

Once they graduate from high school, home schoolers closely parallel their public school counterparts, whether they pursue more formal education or enter the job market (Figure 19.0).

This study demonstrates that home schooling works. It suggests that direct parental involvement and hard work are the keys to educational success. Regardless of race, gender, socioeconomic status,

What Happens After Graduation?

Figure 19.0

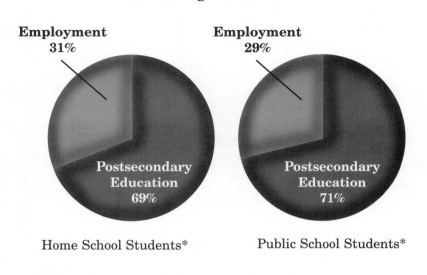

Home School Students*   Public School Students*

* Percentages do not include military, unemployed, missions, ministry, volunteer work, etc., since these categories were not available for both groups.

Public school graduate data based on table from National Educational Longitudinal Survey (NELS) 1988–1994 Descriptive Summary Report. Washington, DC: U.S. Department of Education.

---

parent education level, teacher certification, or the degree of government regulation, the academic achievement scores of home educated students significantly exceed those of public school students. Home school students are fully engaged in society and experience a wide range of opportunities outside the home. They are smart users of both technology and their time. And graduates are equipped to pursue their aspirations—work or college. Contrary to the often speculative opinions of critics, the facts from this study demonstrate success.

The
Future of
Home
Schooling

1

Classical Education Comes Home

H ome schooling parents have the same kind of educational aspirations for their children as other parents. We want our children to have a solid grounding in the basics of learning. We want our children to be able to think logically and to present their thoughts in coherent prose and speech. We want our children to understand the history of our nation and the roots of our culture. We want our children to master the tools of learning so that they can meet the challenges of adult life. And we especially want our children to integrate and test all knowledge and learning against the values and worldview that we, as parents, hold.

The vast majority of home schooling parents also want their children to embrace biblical values and a Christian worldview. Some home schoolers adhere to other value systems, but they, like virtually all parents, hope their children will accept the values they have chosen for their family.

In the early 1980s a few thousand brave parents looked at the multiple choices available for their children and decided to select "none of the above." Instead, they chose home schooling because the alternatives available had failed to deliver an education that was consistent with their aspirations.

The result has been phenomenal. Home schooled children now number 1.2 million strong in the United States—and that number is steadily growing. And the academic achievement of home schooled children far surpasses that of any of the alternatives. In the latest and largest national study, home school children scored on average at the 87th percentile on the composite battery of nationally normed standardized achievement tests. That is 37 percentile points higher than the national average for public schools.

But many experienced home schooling parents have a vague sense that there is yet more that can be done to fulfill the dreams they have for their children. I believe that the "something more" that many home schooling parents are looking for is *classical education*. Our movement loves to recite the fact that George Washington, Patrick Henry, and John Quincy Adams were home schooled for all or a significant part of their education. We want our children to become like these men when they are grown. But we need to realize that the success of these men was not due solely to the methodology of home schooling. The content of their studies was important as well. They were grounded in the three R's. They were taught formal courses in Latin and logic. They read the great literature that has shaped our culture. They knew history—both facts and meaning. They were taught to speak and write and debate. And it was all wrapped in a package that reinforced the Christian worldview.

The modern home schooling movement is poised to take its second great step. We have already embraced the right methodology and many of the components of the kind of education that Patrick Henry received from his father. In the next five to ten years, I believe that tens of thousands of home schooling families will embrace the balance of Patrick Henry's education by adopting the intellectual rigors, emphasis on logic and presentation skills, and worldview training that comprise classical education.

Let's practice a little logic right now and look over the sequence of events that has led us to this point of great opportunity for academic and moral excellence.

The Dangers of Modern Public Education

Most home schooling families have chosen this form of education because of the dangers of the public schools—academic failure, moral decay, and physical safety. One home schooling mother told me that she had made the decision after her daughter's dress had been ripped open by a male classmate. Many parents have reported threats and physical assaults on their children to public school officials only to be told that they are powerless to protect the children. One California family began home schooling when their elementary schoolchild came home with rope burns on his neck. His classmates had tried to hang him!

For Christian parents, the assault on our values is yet another reason to flee the public schools. We were appalled when an organization named Hot, Sexy, and Safer Productions, Inc, showed up at a high school and demonstrated how to use a condom. The now-infamous episode in East Stroudsburg, Pennsylvania, in 1996, when a group of sixth-grade girls were forcibly given vaginal examinations over their tearful objections, exemplifies the stark difference between the moral values of the education establishment and those held by parents.

Our religious values are also accosted in public school practices. We don't like it when the Pilgrims in a seventh grade textbook thank only the Indians and leave God out of the picture (I came across this problem in the eighties when I was a lawyer for Concerned Women for America). An even worse example is a case I handled against the Mead School District in Washington State in which the students were required to read a textbook that called Jesus Christ "a long-legged white s— of a b—."

Parents also place great value on academic achievement. We are painfully aware of the failures in basic learning. I once testified in a federal hearing following Albert Shankar, president of America's second largest teachers' union. His assessment was that 75 percent of the high school graduates of this country were functionally illiterate—as measured by their inability to rank order basic fractions or write a standard business letter.

The dumbing down of public education starts with the textbooks.

Once, during a lawsuit in Tennessee, I had to take the depositions of the top editors for a reading series published by Holt, Rinehart & Winston, which was being used in thousands of New York City public schools. I wanted to compare the original stories with the edited versions that were printed in the reading texts. Editors call this "editing for readability." I particularly remember a story set in Africa from which editors had removed the word "antelope" and substituted "deer." When I asked the New York City editor if this was an example of "dumbing down textbooks," she replied, "No, since there are no antelopes in America, we didn't think the children needed to read that word." People in Wyoming will be surprised to learn that there are no antelopes in America. And didn't New York City book editors ever sing "Home on the Range"? Dumbing down starts at the highest levels.

Unfortunately, this kind of education genuinely hampers the ability of students to succeed in their adult lives. A clerk at the local Sears, a recent high school graduate, looked me in the eye one day and said, "Mister, how do you spell 'road'?" On another occasion, the cashier at McDonald's, also a product of our esteemed public education system, saw by her register that she was to give me 88 cents in change. Looking at a drawer full of coins, she paused and haltingly dug out eight dimes and eight pennies—apparently, this was the only way she could figure out how to give me the right change.

While promoting trendy or sentimental worldviews, our public schools—full of physical and moral danger—have given up on reading, writing, and arithmetic. It is little wonder that parents have begun to look seriously at other alternatives for their children's education.

More and more parents now choose home education because of its strengths, not merely because of the dangers and weaknesses of public education. These problems cause them to consider other options, but they choose home education mainly because of a phenomenon I have called "The Great Kid/Average Parent Syndrome." Parents look at other children who have been home schooled and say, "Boy, those are great kids. I'd like my children to turn out like that." And then they look at the parents and say, "They're just average parents. If they can do it successfully, so can I."

There is little question that home schooled children are doing very well indeed compared to their public school counterparts. But, as parents, we should not be satisfied with doing better than a system that, on average, has totally failed to deliver quality academics in a safe atmosphere. We want our children to achieve both academically and morally at the highest levels rather than merely being better than the competition. It is this yearning in the hearts of successful parents that is going to lead many home schoolers in the next five to ten years to include the main components of classical education into their children's education.

What is Classical Education?

Classical education includes study of the Great Books. It involves learning languages, both ancient and modern. And it includes the formal study of logic, together with persuasive writing and speech. But there is a form and order to these subjects whereby a teaching parent can take his or her child through these subjects and see that the child is not only grounded in Western civilization, academic rigor, and biblical thinking, but is also able to defend and expound upon his knowledge and values in a manner that is both convincing and pleasing.

The "patron saint" of most advocates of classical education is Dorothy Sayers. Her 1947 essay "The Lost Tools of Learning" is considered the manifesto of the movement. Sayers is perhaps best known for her popular detective stories, but she was also a scholar of the Middle Ages, translator of Dante's *The Divine Comedy*, author of innumerable radio plays, and a devout Christian who belonged to a brilliant group of Oxford Christians that included theologian-scholar of seventeenth-century literature C.S. Lewis, Hobbit-creator J.R.R. Tolkien, and novelist Charles Williams.

What is the purpose of education? Miss Sayers argues that a good education teaches men and women how to learn for themselves. "For the sole true end of education," she wrote, "is simply this: to teach men how to learn for themselves, and whatever instruction fails to do this is effort spent in vain." An advocate of classical education, Miss Sayers argues that if we are to have a form of education that "preserves intellectual freedom amid complex pressures of our modern society," then "we must turn back the wheel of progress some four or five hundred years." This idea is nothing short of anathema to most of today's trendy educators!

"What use is it to pile task upon task and prolong the days of labor, if at the close the chief object [of education] is left unattained?" Sayers asks. To attain the object of education—which is really learning how to learn—Miss Sayers proposes that we turn back the clock and consider the trivium and the quadrivium, the two categories into which the seven arts of a "liberal education" (or education of a free man) are divided. The trivium generally correlates to our present primary and secondary education and is composed of grammar, rhetoric, and logic (or dialectic). The quadrivium relates more to the university level and, therefore, is beyond the scope of our current discussion.

> **Home schooled children now number 1.2 million strong in the United States—and that number is steadily growing.**

Although Sayers remains the number one guide for classical education, I am also deeply impressed with the work of a young man named Fritz Hinrichs, author of a provocative essay entitled, "Why Classical Education?" When I read Hinrichs's description of classical education, I said to myself, "This is what most home schoolers really want for their children."

It was once the approach favored in most schools. Hinrichs explains why this kind of education was lost in our nation's public schools. "The study of the great books has been the backbone of good education for centuries," he wrote. "If you look at the books that the intellectual giants have read who have arisen in our culture, you will find that there are particular books that come up again and again. These books were required of schoolboys until the rise of Dewey and the democratization of education through the public school system. The public school system saw these books as elitist and not easily comprehensible by the masses and therefore not appropriate for public education."

It was Hinrichs, a graduate of St. John's College—the "great books" school in Annapolis, Maryland—who introduced me to Sayers's seminal article. Unlike the politically correct educators who don't see the virtues of studying Shakespeare instead of rap music, Hinrichs unequivocally states, "Some books are more worthy of study than others because of the profundity and clarity with which they explore the ideas they contain."

Hinrichs is headmaster of the San Diego–based Escondido Tutorial program, which makes his courses available online by computer to home schoolers across the nation. He also upholds the concept of an education steeped in Christian values. But he notes that Christian parents have all too often neglected this greatest gift:

> Christian education has become something of a lost science. Not only have Christians done very little to prepare their children to become godly intellects, but intellectual incompetence has been seen as the true helpmate of vital spirituality. A soft mind has been seen as a vital tool in the pursuit of a soft heart. In our day, mental rigor and a vigorous intellectual pursuit have become equated with doctrinal rigidity and cold spirituality. However, by God's grace, with the increasing interest in classical education, we are seeing a revival of the Christian intellectual tradition.

To get some idea of the intellectual rigor that Hinrichs believes that twelve- to eighteen-year-old home schoolers should undertake, consider his six-year "Great Books" program offered through Escondido Tutorial Service. It takes students through the following steps: (1) Greek history and literature such as Homer and Sophocles; (2) Roman history and literature such as Plutarch and Virgil; (3) Medieval history and literature, including Augustine, Aquinas, and Chaucer; (4) the Renaissance and Reformation, studying the literature of Machiavelli, Calvin, Shakespeare, and Milton's *Paradise Lost*; (5) the Enlightenment and the American and French Revolutions, studying the writings of Locke and Adam Smith, and (6) recent history (relatively speaking), including the Civil War, Napoleon, and German political history while reading the writings of de Toqueville, Tolstoy, and C.S. Lewis.

But the story of Western civilization and the great books are only one component of classical education—the courses offered by Hinrichs illustrate the level of accomplishment that is possible. Let's go back to the beginning of classical education and see how the building blocks fit together.

The Three Stages of the Trivium

As we mentioned earlier, classical education is generally divided into two main components, the trivium (primary and secondary education) and the quadrivium (university training). The trivium is composed of three subparts: Grammar, Dialectic, and Rhetoric. The Grammar stage teaches basic facts and skills, the Dialectic stage steeps children in logic and helps to teach them the reasoning behind many of the facts they learned in the Grammar period, and the Rhetoric stage focuses on the children's ability to present their worldview in a pleasing and logical manner. In simple terms Grammar teaches facts, Dialectic teaches reasoning, and Rhetoric teaches presentation.

The Grammar Stage

After the basic skills of reading, writing, and math are begun, the child is ready at about age nine to launch into the Grammar stage of the Trivium. During the Grammar stage of life, "children possess a great natural ability to memorize large amounts of information even though they may not understand its significance," Hinrichs observes. He continues, "This is the time to fill them full of facts, such as the multiplication table, geography, dates, events, plant and animal classifications; anything that lends itself to easy repetition and assimilation by the mind." I would add that this is a great time to encourage children to memorize numerous and even lengthy passages from the Bible.

Both Sayers and Hinrichs strongly encourage the study of Latin or Greek during the Grammar period. Although I have not studied either, I believe that Latin has much to offer. For starters, Latin is an inflected language, which means that the endings of words tell how they are used in the sentence. This will be of enormous help in learning how to use the English language.

Miss Sayers argues for Latin in the following terms:

> I will say at once, quite firmly, that the best grounding for education is the Latin grammar. I say this, not because Latin is traditional and medieval, but simply because even a rudimentary knowledge of Latin cuts down the labor and pains of learning almost any other subject by at least 50 percent. It is the key to the vocabulary and structure of all the Teutonic languages, as well as to the technical vocabulary of all the sciences and to the literature of the entire Mediterranean civilization, together with all its historical documents.

Miss Sayers also argues for the study of a modern foreign language during the Grammar stage. I heartily endorse this idea, although I realize that the practical difficulties for home schooling parents to teach either Latin or a modern foreign language can be considerable. (I'll offer some ideas on overcoming such difficulties as we move along.)

Some may be concerned about the emphasis on memorizing a great many facts during the Grammar stage. But children need to memorize the basic facts of grammar, history, geography, art, addition, subtraction, multiplication, and division simply because they are the necessary tools for further learning.

Dorothy Sayers defends memorization during the Grammar period by saying:

> [A]nything and everything which can be usefully committed to memory should be memorized at this period, whether it is immediately intelligible or not. The modern tendency is to try and force rational explanations on a child's mind at too early an age. Intelligent questions, spontaneously asked, should, of course, receive an immediate and rational answer; but it is a great mistake to suppose that

a child cannot readily enjoy and remember things that are beyond his power to analyze.

Remember, students are not being encouraged to memorize and master this material as an end in itself, but to lay a foundation for life-long learning.

The Dialectic Stage

Around age eleven, most children are ready to move on to the second stage of classical education—the Dialectic. In the first stage, we focused on the child's observation and memory. In this stage the emphasis is on a child's ability to engage in discursive reason. "It is during this stage," Hinrichs writes, "that the child no longer sees the facts that he learned as merely separate pieces of information but he starts to put them together into logical relationships by asking questions. No longer can the American Revolution merely be a fact in history but it must be understood in the light of the rest of what the child has learned."

A formal course in logic is ideal at this stage of a child's education. It is time to teach cause and effect, steps of reasoning, and how to make proper inferences.

The sentence most used by a teaching parent during the Dialectic period should be, "Why do you say that?" Our children should be taught to present a logical and defensible explanation for every assertion they make. If your child writes an essay that proclaims, "America is the greatest nation on earth," he should be prepared to defend his conclusion. Current events are useful for starting your discussion and debate.

There are strong reasons for including a formal course in logic in our children's education. We want our children to be able to think clearly and present their arguments cogently. Sometimes we seem intent on crushing our child's propensity to argue because it appears to be a sign of rebellion. While undisciplined argumentativeness is not appropriate, a child's ability to present a logical argument in support of a biblical worldview is a tremendous asset. We can defend our faith better if we know how to reason, think, and evaluate information.

After all, do we want our children to be tools of popular culture or intelligent critics of it? We need to take our children's natural tendency to argue and channel it to good critical purposes.

Commercial advertising will have you believe that every man will be perceived as incredibly sexy by gorgeous young women if only he will drink the right soft drink or right beer or drive the right car. If this kind of manipulation didn't work, the companies wouldn't run the ads. A classical education that emphasizes reason, logic, and good taste can inoculate our children against this kind of commercial puffery or the worst political manipulation.

We want our children to be able to argue politely and civilly, of course. We don't want them to be smart alecks who blurt out their opinions or children who are rude or disrespectful of their elders. But Miss Sayers points out:

> It will, doubtless, be objected that to encourage young persons at the pert age to browbeat, correct, and argue with their elders will render them perfectly intolerable. My answer is that children of that age are intolerable anyhow; and that their natural argumentativeness may just as well be canalized to good purpose as allowed to run away into the sands. It may, indeed, be rather less obtrusive at home if it is disciplined in school; and anyhow, elders who have abandoned the wholesome principle that children should be seen and not heard have no one to blame but themselves.

The heaviest academic content for the Dialectic period should be the study of the Great Books, blending a study of literature with the relevant historical periods. A student should learn ancient Greek history at the same time he is reading the *Iliad* and the *Odyssey* so that the issues and the events presented in the literature can be both understood and debated in their historical context.

During the Dialectic period the goal is to shape lessons so that they fit a coherent whole and are not merely disjointed studies presented without coherence.

The Rhetoric Stage

"During this period," writes Hinrichs, speaking of fourteen- to sixteen-year-olds, "the child moves from merely grasping the logical sequence of arguments to learning how to present them in a persuasive, aesthetically pleasing form." Dorothy Sayers also calls this period the Poetic age, because during this period "the student develops the skill of organizing the information he has learned into a well-reasoned format that will be both pleasing and logical.

Sometimes I think we could all use some training in presenting our arguments felicitously. I've noticed that some "movement conservatives" stopped their development at the Dialectic stage. They are good at analyzing issues and events. But they lack the ability to write or speak well and aren't polite in argument. At times I've been guilty of slugging it out like a prize fighter myself. Fortunately, my wife Vickie usually sets me straight. After one particularly fierce verbal free-for-all on a television talk show, she counseled, "Mike, you need to remember that you're really trying to win the people listening at home. To gain their support, your message has to be like hearing a song. You need to get the words right—and you usually do—but you have to sing a sweet melody as well."

In the Rhetoric stage children should be asked two questions, "How can you say that more clearly?" and, "How can you say that in a manner your audience will find more pleasing?"

Miss Sayers begins her discussion of the third stage of the Trivium with this somewhat vague description:

> It is difficult to map out any general syllabus for the study of Rhetoric: a certain freedom is demanded. In literature, appreciation should be again allowed to take the lead over destructive criticism; and self-expression in writing can go forward, with its tools now sharpened to cut clean and observe proportion. Any child who already shows a disposition to specialize should be given his head: for, when the use of the tools has been well and truly learned, it is available for any study whatever.

In my opinion, home schooling is the only form of education that has the flexibility to bring to students the kind of individualization that Sayers espouses. Students who are inclined toward the sciences and mathematics should be encouraged to begin their specialization, while still studying some literature and history. And the reverse is true for those gifted in the humanities. "The scope of Rhetoric," Sayers says, "depends also on whether the pupil is to be turned out into the world at the age of sixteen or whether he is to proceed to the university."

Although it is my experience that many of our home-schooled children aspire to careers in the "public square," not all of them will. Some won't want to become ministers, lawyers, statesmen, or journalists. Not everyone requires the same degree of polished rhetorical skills so essential in the public arena. But all adults need to be able to communicate ideas and information in a rational and pleasing manner. Such skills are useful in any job, in situations as diverse as talking to an appliance repairmen or interacting with other members of a church board.

The Need for a Christian Worldview

Some components of classical education may leave a lot of experienced home schoolers—especially Christians—with a few nagging doubts. The leaders of the Renaissance, which embraced humanism and rationality to the exclusion of the Christian faith, were predominantly educated in the classical manner, with a heavy influence of Greek and Roman philosophers. Our goal is not to produce a New Renaissance. We want our children to be more like the leaders of the Reformation, who were also schooled in the classical style. The leaders of the Renaissance received the Greek and Roman thought as truth, while the leaders of the Reformation took certain lessons from ancient history and then superimposed the teachings of Scripture over them.

I would not be interested in any classical program for my own children unless it was founded on a solidly Christian worldview. Yes, I would like my children to read Plato, but not in order to adopt Plato's views in most areas. Rather, by understanding what Plato said, they can grasp both how it influenced society and how it can refute the errors that Plato injected into the philosophy of Western civilization.

Christian classical education is not neutral. It takes definite philosophical sides. And all that is old is not necessarily good.

Not only should classical material be read through the critical eyes of a Christian, but care should be taken to ensure that our students read more material that is positive and reinforces our views rather than competing views.

Additionally, classical education must be Americanized to some considerable extent if we are going to do our job of producing leaders for this country. Yes, we are a part of Western civilization, but we live in a particular branch of that civilization. A heavy dose in the literature and history of the Founding Fathers as well as the writings of great Americans in the intervening years must be included to make a truly ideal program for the modern American home schooler.

Some of the Best Material on the Market

In addition to the courses offered by Escondido Tutorial Services, one of the best programs I have seen that offers a clearly Christian classical education is David Quine's *World Views of the Western World*, published by the Cornerstone Curriculum Project. *World Views* is a three-year program that is built largely around the works of Francis Schaeffer. Students still read Homer, Socrates, and Machiavelli. But these are balanced not only by Schaeffer's works, but also by St. Augustine, Luther, and Calvin. Cornerstone's *World Views* is in its first edition and has many good features in place that make it quite usable for most home schooling mothers who don't have the time to sit and read classical literature for fifteen to twenty hours a week.

And Quine plans to make the program even more user friendly. While students will be required to read the entire work of *The City of God* by Augustine, for example, Quine is developing a parent's guide to the book which allows a parent to read an hour or so of selections from it and fill in the balance with Quine's own summaries. Most parents would devote this hour a week to enable them to guide their children successfully through Cornerstone's clear lesson plans, daily questions, and quizzes. Quine also employs a number of videos that are great teaching tools for making history and literature come alive—the movie *Gettysburg*, for example, plus presentations by Schaeffer.

World Views is academically challenging, Christian-based, and provides a good exposure to classical literature, history, art, and music. It is superior to almost all high schools, as well as to the liberal arts components offered in most colleges and universities. The cost for all books, materials, videos, lesson plans, and tests is about $600 for the first year, and about $350 for each of the following years. Many home schooling families will already have a number of

More and more parents now choose home education because of its strengths, not merely because of the dangers and weaknesses of public education.

the necessary books and materials in their personal libraries, which will reduce their costs substantially.

But a parent will need to add to *World Views*—not only mathematics, science, and foreign language, but also much more in speaking skills and formal logic. No program has all the elements of an ideal classical system. But it seems clear that all of the components will be in place in the next three to five years.

Any successful course material will pass the number one litmus test for home schoolers: *Is it easy for the parent to use?* Quine's plan calls for a student to spend fifteen to twenty hours a week on the material, while a parent would spend four to seven hours in preparation, instruction, and discussion. This kind of ratio will enable thousands of home schooling mothers to offer an intense, academically challenging course while keeping her sanity with all her other duties. In talking with Quine, I believe he has caught the vision to make his materials even easier in the years ahead.

Four other programs which offer important aspects of classical education deserve some special recognition.

Calvert School, the nation's oldest home school provider, is recognized among classic education fans as providing a good program that contains many classical elements. Calvert offers courses only from kindergarten through eighth grade. Also, Calvert is not a specifically Christian program. But a number of Christian friends who use the program tell me that its worldview supports traditional themes of Western civilization. It's definitely worth a look.

Konos, which is the granddaddy of unit study programs, also has a classical flavor in many of its materials. Many thousands of mothers are thrilled with Konos, although some believe it requires a great deal of work. Jessica Hulcy, Konos's inspiration, is a dynamic woman with great vision and is constantly updating her program, making it even more academically appropriate as well as teacher-friendly. If you are interested in this approach, you should examine Konos for sure. Konos has been heavily weighted toward the K-8 years as well.

A newcomer, Progeny Press, offers a simple, easy-to-use guide to teaching great literature from a Christian perspective. This program is inexpensive, and while not a comprehensive classical program, certainly gives students in all grades a good exposure to many great books, and uses them to reinforce a Christian worldview and critical thinking.

A good friend and longtime home schooler, Rob Shearer is also offering a number of important books through his Greenleaf Press, which should be considered by anyone wanting to pursue great books or classical studies. Some of his titles include: *Famous Men of the Renaissance & Reformation*, *Famous Men of the Middle Ages*, *Famous Men of Greece*, *Famous Men of Rome*.

A final resource that is an absolute must is not a curriculum as such, but a resource center for Christian home schoolers interested in classical education. *Trivium Pursuit* is a magazine and resource center that offers teaching guides, book lists, practical instruction, and tapes that give many aspects of the whys and hows of classical education. *Trivium Pursuit* embraces a traditional classical approach which advocates Latin, Greek, and formal logic, as well as great books. Harvey and Laurie Bluedorn are home schooling parents who offer their own success with classical education to many others through written materials and seminars.

Needed Adaptations

In this chapter I have predicted that classical education will become a major choice among home schoolers. But that will happen only if those who are interested in making this kind of curriculum available consider a number of adaptations that will make the approach both acceptable and realistically accessible to home schoolers.

The kind of classical education program that can dominate the home schooling market must include the following components and features:

■ *Core curricula aids designed for teaching parents.* The basis of the core curricula is the classic literature of Western civilization. But for parent home schoolers, the Great Books need to be accompanied by succinct, meaningful teaching parent guides specifically designed for the home schooling market, emphasizing how this material fits into the overall scheme of classical education. These guides must give the parent the direction he or she needs to read selected portions of these books simply to save time. She needs to be able to do an hour (or less) of preparation to give her child four hours (or more) of work.

■ *Classical "coaches" on call or on-line.* Almost no home schooling parents were tutored in the Great Books or Euclidian geometry. Seminars in "teaching classical education" need to be offered by experienced instructors at every home schooling conference. And parents need and deserve help on a continuing basis. I believe that parents will pay top dollar for a service that offers a combination of books, teacher's manuals, initial training, and ongoing support in delivering comprehensive classical education.

■ *An American studies curriculum.* The classical education programs I have examined deal with the roots of Western civilization extensively, while considering American civilization, history, and literature only a fraction of the time. But if we are to turn out good and thoughtful citizens, we should emphasize American history.

■ *High-tech foreign language instruction.* Most home schooling parents will gladly accept assistance in teaching their children a foreign language—whether it is a classical language like Latin or Greek, or a modern language like French, Spanish, or Russian.

It is best to learn a foreign language from a native speaker. The second best is to learn from a person who is completely fluent in the language.

We have purchased a video series called "Muzzy," produced by the British Broadcasting Company, that teaches French. This same program is available in a number of other languages as well. It is an interesting program of cartoons, and the children like it, at least for a while. But the Muzzy series offers only a handful of lessons. What is really needed, if cartoons are to be the instructional tool, are dozens and dozens of episodes.

I believe that truly high-tech foreign language instruction is just around the corner. In fact, the technology is already here. Via the internet or telephone hookups, two-way online verbal conversations are possible. Learning a foreign language well not only requires the student to hear the teacher—the teacher must also be able to hear the student and respond. In larger metropolitan areas foreign language instruction is already offered in home schooling support groups and satellite programs. These programs will continue to flourish.

The greatest strain on many home schooling families is the pressure of time. And often it is just too difficult to cart one's twelve-year-old off to her Spanish lesson when a home schooling mother has four younger students she has to teach and care for. Thus the more foreign language instruction that can be offered by video, computer, or other forms of technology, the greater the home schooling market.

■ *Debate teams through satellite schools or support groups.* There is no doubt about the value of learning to debate. Debating is quite different from arguing. Debate requires organization, facts, rational presentation, and a neutral judge. Argument requires only emotion and an opinion.

Home schooling support groups are quite capable of organizing and running debate teams. Satellite programs that offer local assistance on curricular matters will also develop their own debate programs in the near future.

There may be some frustration with attempts to join the public school's debate leagues. Public schools might do one-on-one competitions with a home school team as an exhibition, but high school league rules will get in the way of many desired interactions.

The good news is that there are now enough home school support groups as well as home schooled students ages twelve and older to be able to participate in a debate outside the public school arena. Debate should not be limited to high schoolers. I would strongly urge the inclusion of all those in the Dialectic stage of their studies.

I see the value of debate not only from my own experience in high school, college, and law school but also from the experience of my daughter Christy. She has joined one of the best college debate teams in the nation, based on her home schooling experience.

One of the best things about debate is that one must argue both sides of the issue. In the first round of a tournament a debater favors the proposition, and in the second round he opposes the same proposition. This is not instilling wishy-washyness in a student. Rather, it teaches a valuable lesson in understanding competing arguments.

Home school debate teams require only two people. A large institutional high school is simply not necessary. But coaching is essential, and it has proved helpful when experienced home schooling debaters hold coaching clinics from time to time.

Forensics competitions are a vital part of a classical education. "Oratory" competitions involve giving a polished persuasive speech of about seven minutes. "Extemporaneous speaking" requires a person to give a speech about a minute after being handed a card with a topic on it. "Oral interpretation" requires a presentation of a piece of drama, poetry, or literature. Any time a student gets in front of an audience and talks, it is a good thing—especially if he or she is critiqued appropriately afterward.

A Better Education in Less Time

You may have noticed that the last stage of the trivium is designed to end around age sixteen. That is two years earlier than the completion age for the less rigorous public education course of studies.

Public school education takes too long; John Quincy Adams entered Harvard at the age of fourteen. I see no reason why a youngster today can't move either toward the university or the world of work at a much earlier age than is now the norm.

Sayers suggests that we should be alarmed, not comforted, that students are in school much longer today than in the days of the Tudors. In those days, students routinely entered the university system in their midteens. Students were "held fit to assume responsibility for the conduct of their own affairs." Sayers asks, "Are we altogether comfortable about that artificial prolongation of intellectual childhood and adolescence into the years of physical maturity?"

I have long believed that junior high is a complete waste of time. Examine any seventh or eighth grade math book. You will find the vast majority of the work to be nothing more than additional problems to relearn mathematical skills taught in the fifth and sixth grades. One learns American history in the eighth grade in most public schools, a subject which is normally repeated in the eleventh grade. It would be comforting if eleventh grade American history were somehow intellectually more challenging than the eighth grade variety, but even when I took these subjects more than thirty years ago, there was little difference in either the depth or scope of the courses. In my own case, my eighth grade teacher gave a course much more on the college level to a group of thirteen-year-old honor students. History in the eleventh grade was simply a bore by comparison. We were ready for much greater challenges.

Some educators have admitted to me that the junior high school years are basically repetitions of what the child has previously learned. The real purpose of junior high, I have been told, is to provide an intellectually less stimulating time so that the child can negotiate the emotional turmoil of puberty.

Students who are truly capable of university-level scholarship are also capable of getting there about three years earlier than is typical under the current educational regime. I know this from personal experience. When our second daughter, Jayme, was about to enter the seventh grade, I examined the seventh grade math and history texts that were a continuation of her sixth grade program. They were a virtual repetition of the previous year's work. I looked over another publishing house's offerings and found the same thing. So Jayme, taught primarily by my wife Vickie (who likes to joke that she overcame the handicap of a major in education to be able to teach), skipped two grades.

She graduated from high school at age fifteen. Was she adequately prepared? The National Merit Scholarship folks certainly thought so. Jayme was a Commended Scholar in the National Merit Scholarship program. And did home schooling make Jayme afraid to venture out into the world? Hardly. A graphic artist by training, Jayme is now in Romania, where she is broadening her horizons through the moving experience of working in a Rumanian orphanage. Jayme was ready for the adult world of work (via apprenticeship) or a university before she was old enough to drive.

We also feel that Christy, our oldest daughter, is a home schooling success story, if you'll excuse a proud father's bragging. Her story also demonstrates the ability to handle adult responsibility at a younger age. At seventeen, she was the principal press officer during my campaign for lieutenant governor of Virginia. She regularly dealt with the national and local media with such maturity that reporters generally assumed that she was a college graduate. Christy is now a student at Cedarville College, a Christian liberal arts school in Ohio, where she maintains a 3.9 grade point average and is vice president of the student body.

Many youngsters, however, aren't cut out for advanced academic work, and maybe it's time for society to face this reality. These young people aren't well served by being forced to remain in school after age fifteen or sixteen. This does not mean that these students should not learn the material offered in high school. I believe that they should learn at least this level, if not substantially more challenging material, but that they should do so by the time they finish the eighth grade. We have to realize that something is dreadfully wrong with a system that forces illiterate fifteen-year-olds to remain in large institutions for three more years when they finally emerge just as illiterate.

We face even greater alarms from the totalitarian measures that elected officials and educational bureaucrats are willing to impose to force these unwilling students to remain in school. We deny driver's licenses to dropouts. We impose daytime curfews on the law-abiding as well as the lawless. We deny work permits to those who prefer to work rather than study.

We send these young people the message that they are too young to accept adult responsibilities for study and work. (Ironically, at the same time we tell them that premarital sex is perfectly okay, as long as they use a condom.) How much better for these young people if they were allowed to get into the world and assume responsibility for their own lives! A young man who has entered an apprenticeship program at fifteen will likely be ready to support a family three to five years later.

We need not look only to the Middle Ages or an isolated home schooler to show that it is not necessary to prolong basic education to eighteen years of age. Switzerland, one of the most advanced nations in the world, offers us an up-to-date example. Approximately 75 percent of Swiss students finish their academic studies for good at the end of the equivalent of our eighth or ninth grade. Somewhere between the ages of fourteen and sixteen they enter into an apprenticeship program. (And these programs are not just for blue collar jobs. Two of the three largest banks in the world are headed by men who entered into banking through their company's apprenticeship programs at this young age.) The 25 percent of Swiss students who go to high school are roughly the same group that go on to university. The Swiss people are both highly educated and highly successful, boasting the highest per capita income of any nation in the world.

If we can allow our children to progress at a better pace, cutting out the time wasted by repetition, we will have gone a long way toward restoring education to its proper function: the function of teaching people how to learn. This is one of the reasons I am so sold on classical education.

I firmly believe that, if home schoolers adopt the curriculum outline (as modified) of the trivium together with its organizational plan, we will achieve our aspirations of raising young men and women who are truly as capable as Patrick Henry. We will earn a great spot in history if we can train the next generation of great leaders that this nation so desperately needs.

2

Broadening Our Political Horizons

W̶e home schoolers were forcibly thrust into the political fray from the moment of the birth of our movement in the early 1980s. One of the first questions we were asked was: *Is that legal?* Unfortunately, it was a question frequently asked by dubious prosecutors and judges.

There was no choice. If we hadn't learned to work in the political process to gain legislation which recognized a greater measure of our God-given and constitutionally protected rights, the movement would have been limited to those hardy souls who were willing to risk an almost inevitable trip before a judge, courtesy of the local public school officials.

If the education establishment had been able to gaze into a New Age crystal ball and see the future, they might have quietly consented to the legalization of home education. But they didn't, and the result is that a decade and a half of legal and political persecution have transformed home schoolers into a politically potent force that is beginning to break out of the narrow confines of the interests of home education.

Home schooling parents and children are taking our political movement into a second stage. With our organizations in place ready to do instant battle on any issue that directly threatens home education, thousands of individual parents and older students are becoming some of the most effective political operatives in the nation.

Home schooling organizations are not engaging in new frontiers of activism. These organizations, including the one I lead, have properly kept to their original missions—which still are vitally important, as we shall see. But armed with the experience learned in the battle against the education establishment for the right to home school, home school parents and teens are engaging in battles for human life, limited government, lower taxes, proper foreign policy, and a host of other issues far beyond the concerns on which we cut our political teeth.

> **Within ten years, home schoolers will equal or surpass the NEA in every measurable criterion of political savvy, power, and involvement.**

For now, consider this single snapshot of the growing trend of broadened political involvement. Single-issue activists are rarely selected as delegates to major party conventions. Delegates are chosen from among the ranks who battle in the multi-issue arena of electoral politics.

In 1992 I was one of only about four or five home schoolers who were delegates to the Republican National Convention in Houston. At San Diego's GOP National Convention in 1996, I met at least seventy home schooling delegate parents.

For many years, the National Education Association (NEA) has had tremendous influence in Democratic politics. One of the reasons for this is that thousands of NEA members have broken away from strictly educational issues and become involved in politics at large.

Home schooling parents and teens are rapidly closing in on the NEA in terms of numbers, activity in politics, and the resultant political influence. Within ten years, home schoolers will equal or surpass the NEA in every measurable criterion of political savvy, power, and involvement. This trend will reshape the face of American politics.

Before we consider the current and future implications of broad political involvement, let's look briefly at the history of the battle for home school freedom. This history will help those who didn't live through it to understand both the fervor and the philosophy that brought home schoolers to the threshold of greater activism.

Home Education's Freedom Trail

When my wife and I began home schooling in 1982, only three states—Ohio, Nevada, and Utah—explicitly recognized the right to home school in their state statutes. Washington State, where we lived at the time, was one of the many states that banned home schooling unless the teaching parent had current state teacher's certification.

The word began to pass around the scanty ranks of home schoolers that a lawyer with some experience in First Amendment litigation had joined their ranks with his own family. And the desperate phone calls from parents facing criminal prosecutions began to ring in my office.

It became obvious that the only way home schoolers were going to be able to afford the kind of legal help they needed was by forming an association committed exclusively to their defense. So in March of 1983, with the assistance of J. Michael and Elizabeth Smith, and Jim and Jeannie Carden, Vickie and I formed the Home School Legal Defense Association (HSLDA).

HSLDA was designed as an advocacy group for home schooling families. We provide free legal defense for our members on any matter concerning home education (except in divorce cases). After a family pays its dues of $100 per year, we guarantee them free advice and representation. We will assist nonmember families as well, but only if we believe their case presents a precedent-setting issue.

Since the beginning of our organization we have been able to use our resources both to defend individual families and advance the freedom of all home schoolers in the judicial and legislative arenas.

Many state home schooling organizations were being formed at the same time HSLDA was created. State organizations and HSLDA have been the army and air force team that fight the establishment for parental freedoms. HSLDA is the air force. We flew wherever needed to defend the families who were being charged with truancy or related charges. We also filed a number of affirmative lawsuits in those early days in an attempt to have old state laws banning home education declared unconstitutional.

The first case of this nature was in Washington State. Soon after we filed the case and began taking the depositions of the state superintendent of public instruction and other officials, we reached a quick truce. No more prosecutions of home schoolers would be forthcoming until the legislature had a chance to consider a home schooling bill that was filed soon after we began our lawsuit. In 1985 the Washington legislature passed a new law which was quite lenient for its time and our lawsuit was put in abeyance.

By the end of 1985 home schooling bills had been passed in thirteen other states, most of which had had significant litigation—done by HSLDA or, in many cases, by private attorneys—prior to the passage of the new state law. In every case, the state organizations played the role of the "home school army" and were the significant force that won political victory for their state.

By this time, the relatively easy victories were over. And the home schooling movement settled in for a season of protracted litigation with dozens of simultaneous cases. We had a number of important cases in South Carolina, New York, Pennsylvania, Rhode Island, North Dakota, Michigan, Iowa, and Texas. I kept hoping for a home schooling family from Maui to get in trouble in February, but instead I found myself at that time standing once again in front of the supreme court of North Dakota.

One of my favorite cases from this time in our history illustrates how unreasonable school officials were in their approach to a family's right to educate their children.

Maggie Smeltzer of Curryville, Pennsylvania, was entering the fifth grade—her third year of home schooling—when I got a desperate call from her parents. They had begun home schooling Maggie after a couple of rocky years in the Spring Cove, Pennsylvania, public schools. The public school officials attributed Maggie's low achievement to the fact that she was "borderline learning disabled," according to the school's "experts."

The Smeltzers believed differently and sought approval for their program—under an old Pennsylvania law which allowed local super-intendents total discretion over such requests. Approval was reluctantly granted for two years in a row.

My first question to the Smeltzers was: "Why is the superintendent denying you the right to teach your daughter this year after granting approval for the two prior years?"

Their answer astounded me. Maggie's achievement tests for her second year in home instruction were so high that the school district now believed she was "gifted and talented." And so the local officials concluded that Maggie's parents were incapable of teaching a gifted child and filed criminal charges to force her back into the public schools.

I immediately drafted a federal civil rights lawsuit against the superintendent and the school district. I attached the proposed complaint to a letter which I sent by overnight mail to the district demanding that they dismiss their criminal complaint and immediately approve this family's program. In the letter I asked the obvious question: "What do you want to do? Do you want this girl back in the public schools so you can drag her down to the borderline learning disabled level once again?"

The school officials capitulated the following day and dismissed all charges.

Other superintendents in Pennsylvania continued to make unreasonable demands on home schooling families and so, shortly after resolving the Smeltzer case, we filed a federal civil rights lawsuit on behalf of six other families from all over the state who were experiencing similar harassment.

In 1988 Federal District Judge Edwin M. Kosik ruled that, indeed, Pennsylvania's law that gave each superintendent the unbridled discretion to make up whatever policy he wished was an unconstitutional law that violated the due process rights of home schooling families.

By this time, a bill expanding home schooling freedoms had languished in the Pennsylvania legislature for years. But now that the courts had agreed with the "nuclear attack" which had been launched by the HSLDA "air force," the issue was placed front and center on the legislative agenda.

In the midst of the lobbying efforts led by Howard Richman and Tom Eldridge, a thirteen-year-old girl was called to testify before a legislative committee. She told the story of how her family had been harassed under the old law and asked the legislators to pass this new bill.

One senator asked her, "What do you want to be when you grow up?"

"A constitutional litigator," came the answer from Maggie Smeltzer. Her answer brought down the house and was one of the reasons the Pennsylvania legislature unanimously passed the 1988 home schooling law.

While we had been involved in dozens of cases in Pennsylvania during the years before our federal court victory, only a small percentage of home schoolers were ever required to step into the courtroom to defend their family's education. But in North Dakota, nearly half of all our members were hauled into court in the 1980s.

North Dakota was one of the last three states to have a law that demanded all teachers have a current state teacher's certification. Applied to home schooling, it was an effectual ban for over 95 percent of the families. And the prosecutors in that state were zealous in their efforts to drag every known home schooler into court.

The one North Dakota case that I remember most vividly was heard in Mandan against the family of Mark and Lynette Dagley. The prosecutor in their case decided to use a "scorched earth" approach in order to obtain a criminal conviction. The most reprehensible of his tactics was his decision to subpoena eight-year-old Carrie Dagley to testify against her parents.

Law school didn't come close to preparing me to advise an eight-year-old on how to assert her Fifth Amendment right to refuse to testify against herself. This right was relevant because children, as well as parents, can be criminally prosecuted for truancy.

Carrie was terrified, but as we talked the evening before the trial she did her very best to be brave. But despite her valiant efforts, a few tears escaped from the corners of her eyes, which brought all of my protective instincts into full alert. I told Carrie that if the judge tried to force her to testify against herself or her parents, I would stand in her place and go to jail before I would ever let anything happen to her.

The judge was much more reasonable than the prosecutor and didn't force Carrie to testify. But at the end of the trial, the Dagleys were convicted and we had to file yet another appeal to the Supreme Court of North Dakota. While we won a few technical victories in that court, it repeatedly rejected our arguments that the North Dakota law was unconstitutional.

Even though we lost the case, three things happened that made me believe that each North Dakota defeat—and the Dagley's in particular—had sown seeds for greater victories in the days ahead.

The first of these events involved the Dagleys. Their case attracted national media attention as the phenomenon of home schooling burst upon the national stage. *CBS Evening News* came to film the Dagleys in their home. It was the last story on that evening's broadcast. The story ended, but as the credits began to roll across the screen at the end of the program, you could still see and hear Mark, Lynette, Carrie, and her younger brothers and sisters as they sang in their home. I don't know how many families have a chance to sing *A Mighty Fortress Is Our God* on national television. And I must admit that I shed more tears hearing the

> **Christian Libertarians believe in the maximum freedom possible, bounded by the moral law of God.**

Dagleys sing on TV, than did little Carrie as she struggled with fear the night before she faced an overzealous prosecutor.

We could see the second "seed for future victory" in the fact that even though the state supreme court affirmed conviction upon conviction, no family—including the Dagleys—was ever forced to stop home schooling. They simply paid the somewhat nominal criminal fines and kept right on going, daring the prosecutors to try it again. Legislators noted both the tenacity of our people and the ineffectiveness of the legal system in trying to crush the parental desires for freedom.

The third benefit that arose from the North Dakota case was a heightened degree of national unity among home schoolers. As the legal battles continued, Clinton Birst of the North Dakota Home School Association was able to show real progress in passing home schooling legislation. Clinton and I agreed that the only thing likely to change the minds of state legislators was to shame the state of North Dakota with unwanted national attention.

Home school state leaders from all over the nation flew into Bismarck on a bitterly cold February 20, 1989, for a rally that was to become known as the Bismarck Tea Party. The night before the rally, I suddenly got the "tea idea" and drove to the K-Mart on the north side of Bismarck and purchased every box of Lipton tea bags they had. Through the night, dozens of home schoolers from across America worked to staple a small strip of paper on each bag which read: "The consent of the governed for home schoolers, too!"

Before and after the rally the following morning, we handed thousands of these tea bags to every legislator, state office worker, visitor, and member of the media. Our efforts paid off when, later in 1989, the teacher certification law was repealed and replaced with a better, but far from perfect, substitute that allowed much more parental freedom.

It should not be assumed that the home schoolers' march toward freedom was a straight line going in a winning direction. The NEA and establishment groups passed standing resolutions that demanded reenactment of state certification laws, government control of curriculum choices, and intrusive practices such as home visits. They were also successful in convincing some legislators to try to repeal our hard-won freedoms. But when they tried, we tried harder.

In 1984 Montana passed one of the nation's most lenient home schooling laws. In the ensuing years, the superintendents, school board lobbyists, and other officials constantly grumbled about the recognition of freedom that had been granted to the home schoolers. Finally, in 1991 they decided to try a counterattack by seeking a new law that would impose serious new restraints on what had become home schoolers' accustomed freedoms.

Montana's home schoolers decided that they would fight a two-front war. Not only would they contest the School Board association's proposed legislation but they would also offer a bill of their own. Dubbed the "greater freedom" bill, it would guarantee home schoolers their educational rights on even more favorable terms than did the existing law. Frankly, I was dubious about their chances... but I admired their gumption.

I was invited to testify before the Montana state legislature as these competing bills made their way through the committee system to the floor of each house.

When the day of the hearing arrived, I was deeply impressed with the overflow crowd of home schoolers: more than six hundred home educators packed the hearing room. This was one of the largest crowds to attend a legislative hearing in Montana in recent memory. I testified that the Montana School Board Association's bill would be an unconstitutional violation of the rights of the state's home schoolers. But the biggest event of the day was a nonevent.

Throughout the controversy, the executive director of the School Board Association had repeatedly bragged that he was going to produce a number of "home schooling horror stories" which he was collecting from the superintendents in the state. To his great chagrin, not a single superintendent had sent him even one example of a home schooling failure. Eating his earlier boasts, he was forced to walk to the podium and testify that he had come up empty in his quest to prove the alleged irresponsibility of Montana's home schoolers.

As a result of the strong showing of Montana's home schoolers at the hearing, together with the executive director's embarrassing failure to produce, the legislature voted down the association's bill and passed ours instead. Montana suddenly had the distinction of being the best state in the nation for home school freedoms, though one or two others come pretty close to Montana's high level of freedom.

In early 1993 the supreme court of Michigan closed an important chapter in the persecution of home schooling families when it declared that the nation's last teacher certification was unconstitutional. I had the privilege of arguing that case before the Michigan court for Mark and Chris DeJonge, and thought we had seen the last of serious assaults on our freedoms from teacher certification. Less than a year later, I found out I'd guessed wrong.

The greatest assault on home schooling freedoms almost floated through Congress unnoticed in a nine-hundred-plus–page bill called

H.R. 6, the Elementary and Secondary Education Act of 1994. Congressman George Miller, a regular spokesman for the NEA on the floor of Congress, slipped a provision into this massive bill which required all states to mandate course-specific teacher certification in all schools.

This provision, among other things, would have hurt some public schools, especially small rural schools where the history teacher who happened to be a computer buff couldn't teach a computer science class since his certification wasn't in computer science. The class would have simply been closed. Private schools, which are not required to hire certified teachers in many states, would be forced to fire their teachers with chemistry majors and replace them with teachers who may have known little about chemistry but had taken education courses and were "properly certified."

But, above all, the George Miller provision would have absolutely devastated America's home schooling movement. Only parents who were certified in elementary education could teach students in kindergarten through sixth grade. And from seventh grade on—forget it. A parent would have to be certified in everything—math, science, history, language, the arts, physical education, and so on—in order to home school his or her teens.

Congressman Dick Armey noticed Miller's language in committee and moved to amend the provision to clarify that it applied only to public schools receiving federal funds. Armey's amendment was defeated in committee on a straight party-line vote.

Armey then instructed one of his senior aides, Dean Clancey, to call me and see if we believed that his concerns about the Miller language were valid. It didn't take me long to conclude that Armey's instincts were absolutely right. The provision in H.R. 6 was indistinguishable in its approach and effect from the laws I had battled in Michigan, North Dakota, Iowa, and even Washington State more than a decade earlier.

Home schoolers knew the meaning of teacher certification law and were instantly ready to fight when they heard the news. And fight they did, in a demonstration of political savvy that Washington isn't likely to soon forget.

HSLDA quickly alerted the autonomous state organizations in each of the fifty states about the Miller language and a new amendment that Dick Armey was going to offer on the floor of the House. We also called our own Congressional Action Program coordinators that we had established in most of the 435 congressional districts of the country shortly after the election of Bill Clinton in anticipation of an attack on home schooling freedoms.

Our CAP coordinators and the state leaders called over three thousand local home school support group leaders who then activated their telephone trees to virtually all of America's home educators. And the calls began to pour into the nation's capitol.

Christian and conservative talk radio hosts also rallied to our banner, spreading the word over the air waves. Marlin Maddoux was the first to air the issue nationally, but others soon followed. Beverly LaHaye did several shows on the issue, while Dr. James Dobson of "Focus on the Family" put aside preplanned programs to warn the public about H.R. 6. On Pat Buchanan's syndicated radio program I talked about the proposed legislation and how it would affect home schoolers.

The response of home schoolers, Christian school advocates, and interested friends was historic. Well over a million calls and faxes poured into Congress in the eight days between the first call we received from Dick Armey and the day the vote was taken on the floor of the House.

Newt Gingrich estimated the number of calls to be even greater. A few months later when Gingrich was a guest on the Rush Limbaugh show, he was asked by Rush: "Does it ever really make a difference when people call their representatives about an issue?" "It sure does," Gingrich replied. "You may remember when Dick Armey's home schoolers called on H.R. 6. We got over three million calls, and it really changed the outcome."

When the dust settled, Miller's dangerous language was stripped from the bill by a vote of 422 to 1. Only Miller had the courage to vote for the provision that had already passed in committee. And when Dick Armey's protective language followed for a second vote, it passed 374 to 53—an overwhelming legislative victory.

After the votes were counted, Gary Bauer, president of the Family Research Council and former undersecretary of education in the Reagan administration, said, "The calls on H.R. 6 pouring into Congress far surpassed anything I had ever seen on other issues, including the Clinton tax increase."

The Front Shifts

During the first decade of the modern home schooling movement, an intense battle raged over our right to school our children at home. While this battle still flares up several times a year, the most intense battle of the mid-to-late 1990s has been waged in the murky legal waters of child abuse investigations.

No one is in favor of child abuse. The physical, sexual, and emotional abuse of children is one of the signs of national wickedness. The irony to me is that those who take liberal positions on pornography, drugs, and abortion are often the most strident against child abuse. Maybe someday they will understand that their enthusiasm for these other areas of moral decadence has helped to create a climate where it has become easier for adults to perform absolutely despicable acts against children. The devaluation of the lives of children through abortion has created a culture that believes that children are just a mass of tissue to be disposed of at will by adults—after birth as well as before.

But there is another side of the child abuse crisis in this country. Of the three million reported cases of child abuse each year, 60 percent are "unfounded"—which means there is not even enough evidence to take the social services investigation to the second level of examination. This is far below the evidentiary standard required to even file a case in court, much less gain a conviction for abuse or neglect.

The story that I portray in my novel *Anonymous Tip* (Broadman & Holman 1996) is based on a composite of the cases that I have handled from 1993 to the present at HSLDA.

Hundreds of our member families each year are now facing phony child abuse allegations because some anonymous tipster has decided that home schoolers are a "little strange" and should be investigated.

We have had to defend a mother in Alabama when a tipster whispered into a phone a series of scurrilous allegations: children being allowed to read books in the back seat of the van as mom drove; a three-year-old who still used a bottle; failure to take children for physical exams; and—my personal favorite—the allegation, false, that a ten-year-old boy choked a cat to death.

Both parents, Robert and Maria Kennedy, were home in Los Angeles when a social worker and police officer forced their way in because it had been alleged that the mother had left her children in the family's fenced backyard while she was inside doing housework. (Hello? Is there something wrong with this?)

Once inside, this Los Angeles social worker strip-searched the children, rummaged in the bathroom medicine cabinet, looked in the refrigerator and kitchen cabinets, and demanded medical and school records. The social worker and police team scoured the Kennedy home for over an hour and came up empty.

Shirley Calabretta in Woodland, California, was astonished to find an obstinate social worker at her door one day in October of 1994. Why? An anonymous tipster told a Child Protective Services hotline that she had heard a child's voice yelling "no, no, no" from the backyard. The tipster said that another neighbor also heard (this makes the tip anonymous double hearsay) a child yell "no, Daddy, no."

My children have yelled such things when I have said that it is time to go to bed or clean up their room or hundreds of other innocent things.

The strip search of one of the Calabretta children and the invasion of their home was done on the basis of nothing more than the scantiest rumor that must have been embellished by wild speculation to believe it suggests anything amiss.

These incidents, which I have personally litigated, are from the case files of HSLDA. We have handled similar cases in Louisiana, Texas, New York, and Michigan. And we have convinced social workers who were at the door in virtually every other state that they should leave the family home prior to entry because forcible entry would violate the Fourth Amendment of the U.S. Constitution which prohibits unreasonable searches and seizures.

So far, we have met with reasonably good success in our battle to secure the sanctity of the home of home schooling families. In the Calabretta case, the federal district judge ruled in January 1997 that social workers and police officers must obey the normal rules of the Fourth Amendment when investigating child abuse allegations. This means that child abuse investigators cannot enter a family home unless they have one of the following: (1) a proper warrant issued on probable cause; (2) evidence that rises to the level of probable cause—far more than a mere anonymous tip—that demonstrates that the child is in imminent danger; or (3) the free and knowing consent of the parents.

There is a big difference between an "anonymous tip" and a "confidential report." A confidential report means that the police or social worker knows the identity of the person making the allegation, but keeps his or her name confidential during the investigatory stage. I believe that this is appropriate. But an anonymous tip means that the social worker doesn't even know the name of the person who made the report. Ergo, faceless rumor is sufficient for most social workers to attempt to break through the security of a family's front door. They think they have this power. They are wrong. And HSLDA is on a mission to teach the social workers of America that they need to read and obey the law just like every other government investigator.

More children will be protected if social workers stop investigating so many bogus complaints. There are at least two reasons why the elimination of anonymous tips will help children. First, because social workers are stretched so thin by all of the required investigations, if anonymous callers are screened out more attention will be paid to the 40 percent of the cases that are valid. Second, children who go through a strip search or an interrogation in isolation are traumatized. To a child, a strip search feels much the same as some forms of sexual abuse. The investigator may have the best of motives, but the child is still victimized by this kind of investigation. A better approach is to rescue those who are truly hurting as measured by evidence rather than whispered rumor.

Home schoolers face a greatly disproportionate share of child abuse investigations. Our case files reveal that these investigations were started by disgruntled school officials who were unable to stop families from home schooling directly. Often, the CPS worker is at the door at the behest of an anonymous person who claims to be a neighbor or relative.

No matter how good a state home schooling law is, a family can be subjected to this kind of allegation anywhere in the nation. Fortunately, the Fourth Amendment provides a ready defense all across America.

A Movement Toward Christian Libertarianism

When I was litigating the case in Alabama I described in the last section, my local counsel was an experienced attorney who had been a retired juvenile court judge. He heard my arguments in court and read my briefs with care. We were having lunch during this two-day period when I told him that I was in the process of running for lieutenant governor of Virginia. He was surprised to learn that I am a conservative Republican.

"With all your talk of the Fourth Amendment in this case, I thought you were an ACLU type or something," he told me.

The persecution that home schoolers have endured over the past fifteen years has turned this movement in a decidedly Libertarian direction. As individual home schoolers move into the mainstream political process, we bring the philosophy of Christian Libertarianism to a whole host of issues.

For example, most home schoolers part company with the bulk of the Christian Right on the issue of school prayer. We do not believe that the government should be in the business of taking sides on matters of conscience. This is especially true in a day where the likely school prayer would be: "Dear Earth Mother, Thank you for Al Gore. Amen." While I support student initiated prayer and believe that even official school prayer may be defensible as a matter of constitutional history, the latter practice violates the principles of free will that our faith teaches us.

Most home schoolers do not support vouchers. They believe that their liberty will be diminished wherever government money is expended. Tax credits, which allow parents to keep their own money and never send it to the government in the first place, is a much more popular form of educational choice among home schoolers.

And when our conservative friends try to "get tough on crime," we would be right with them if they were talking about stiffer penalties for those convicted of crimes. But when the crime-fighting tactic is a lessening of the standards of the Fourth Amendment in police searches, our experiences as a persecuted minority lead us to side with groups like the ACLU.

Another major area where home schoolers have broken ranks with other conservatives is in government tracking of identity. In an effort to cut down on illegal immigration, many Republicans and moderate Democrats have proposed that every American citizen be issued a national identity card. I stood at a press conference with representatives of Cesar Chavez and the ACLU and objected to this proposal. Troops and fences at the border? Yes. Identity cards for American citizens? No.

Both the left and the right have people who are willing to coerce the entire American public to obey their whims in areas that liberty suggests be left to the individual.

The growing philosophy of those who have come into the political arena through the home schooling movement places a strong limitation on such coercive measures. Christian Libertarians believe in the maximum freedom possible, bounded by the moral law of God. Abortion, homosexuality, pornography, and drugs violate God's law—so this is where we part company with other Libertarians. But identification cards, taxpayer-sponsored prayer, and unconstitutional police searches violate the rules of freedom—and this is where we part company with some other conservatives.

Home School Activists That Foreshadow the Future

When Maggie Smeltzer told the Pennsylvania legislative committee that she wanted to become a constitutional litigator, she revealed a hope of influencing public policy that burns in a vast number of young people who have been raised in home schooling families. While it was well known in these circles that I had run for office in Virginia in 1993, these young people have many other examples of home schooling parents who have taken a leading role in political affairs.

For me, Maggie's answer represented the future of home schooling. I've noted a large number of home schooling children with similar aspirations. They want to be constitutional litigators, state legislators, city councilmen, congressmen... and more. Meanwhile, their parents are not just sitting around, waiting for the grand day when their children enter the public square. I've already seen a number of these parents jump with both feet into the political arena.

In this connection, I think of people like Tim Lambert, a father and home schooling state leader from Lubbock, Texas. For a number of years Tim has run the Texas Home School Coalition which is the lobbying arm of the home schooling movement in the Lone Star State. Familiar with both the people and process of Texas politics, Tim has taken a real lead in the general world of politics. In the summer of 1996 Tim was elected national committeeman from Texas for the Republican Party. Not content to sit on his laurels, Tim ran for the Texas Senate—a state position that is roughly the same size as a congressional district.

Ricky Boyer is a twenty-one-year-old home school graduate serving his second term as chairman of the Republican Party for Campbell County, Virginia. Ricky was a key volunteer in my own campaign for lieutenant governor of Virginia in 1993. At that time he was just an eighteen-year-old kid with a desire to learn and a great servant's spirit.

The year following my campaign, Ricky decided to challenge the previous Republican County chairman because of the incumbent's liberalism and refusal to work hard for conservative candidates. Ricky, who was then all of nineteen, organized and hustled and shocked the whole state when he successfully beat a middle-aged incumbent for this important party slot.

Two years later, the "moderate" establishment came after Ricky; they weren't going to be taken by surprise this time. Again, young Mr. Boyer, aided by his eleven brothers and sisters, plus a number of other home schoolers among his friends and supporters, fought back. Ricky won, and I doubt that the other side will try again anytime soon.

A number of other adults and older home schooling students are taking a great activist role in politics. Dave Weldon was elected to Congress in 1994 from Florida. Congressman Weldon is a home schooling parent. Mike Thomas, a home schooling father, was the campaign manager for George Allen when he was elected governor of Virginia in 1993. Mike now serves as secretary of administration for Virginia. Ken McKim, a recent home school graduate, ran for the Texas house in 1993. He narrowly lost to a longtime incumbent in his first try for elected office. Daniel Webster, a home schooling father, is the Republican leader in the Florida house of representatives. Republicans took control of the house in 1996, and now Webster will become the Speaker of the Florida house. Another home schooling father, Bob Starks, is also a member of the Florida house. His campaign manager has always been Billy Starks, his home schooling son. Randy Ball, from Bervard County, is yet a third home schooling father serving in the Florida house.

In my campaign for lieutenant governor, there were dozens and dozens of young home schooled kids who learned to pass out literature, ring doorbells, stuff envelopes, make phone calls, raise money, put up yard signs, slap on bumper stickers, and manage the polls on election day. They did all these things, usually standing by their parents' side, and learned practical lessons that will last a lifetime.

But my favorite example of a young home school activist comes from the state of Illinois. A good friend of mine, Penny Pullen, served in the Illinois legislature for a number of years. During one campaign, one of her precinct captains was an eleven-year-old home schooled boy named Jeremy Nerius.

A precinct captain has the responsibility of passing out literature to all the homes in that voting district—usually about five hundred. The captain then calls all the registered voters to determine who favors his or her candidate as well as those leaning in that direction.

Jeremy, at the tender age of eleven, did his job so well that Penny tells me she received a higher percentage of votes in his precinct that any other—ever. But this record was surpassed two years later when Jeremy, working the same precinct at thirteen, achieved an even higher percentage of the vote for Penny. In 1996 Jeremy, then eighteen, was in charge of his city for the U.S. Senate campaign of Al Salvi.

The Madison Project

One of the vehicles that home schoolers will use to advance their political agenda is based on the concept of bundling that the left-wing, pro-abortion Emily's List has used so well. The Emily in Emily's List stands for **E**arly **M**oney **I**s **L**ike **Y**east. This group is committed to giving money to Democratic women candidates for the House and Senate who are committed to the feminist ideology. Emily's List has a significant membership of rich feminist sympathizers who write large checks directly to the candidates. Together, the members of Emily's List give hundreds of thousands of dollars to their endorsed candidates. Traditional PACs can give only $5,000 to a candidate. Emily's List dwarfs that amount in a manner that is perfectly legal and extremely savvy.

Home schoolers are savvy enough to borrow tactics from the opposition. In 1994 I started an organization with a similar methodology, but a completely opposite philosophy. The Madison Project bundles contributions for Republican candidates who are constitutional conservatives. This means they are pro-life, pro-family, pro-Second Amendment, and pro-Tenth Amendment. We have about twenty major issue groups, and a candidate must be good on virtually all of them to get our endorsement and money. We do not give bundled money to any incumbents. It is our belief that they normally have good sources for contributions and someone has to concentrate on new candidates. Madison is also quite willing to take sides in Republican nomination battles—something many PACs won't do.

The Madison Project has a significant home schooling presence in leadership and membership. Our staff is comprised of one home schooling father and three home schooling graduates. But both our board and membership have a significant number of non–home schoolers who play a very active role in the organization. Madison is not a home schooling organization; it is another example of home schoolers playing a significant role in an important political organization within the mainstream of the conservative movement.

In 1994 Madison's members gave $179,000 to nine different candidates for Congress. Five of these challengers won their races. In one race we gave about $20,000 to Andrea Seastrand. She won her election in California by about 1,500 votes. We also gave $15,000 to Mark Neuman from Wisconsin. Congressman Neuman won his election by just 1,100 votes. When we give money to help influence extremely close elections, we really feel as if we are helping to fulfill one of the meanings of the name Madison Project. The word Madison stands for **M**ake **A** **D**ifference **I**n **S**aving **O**ur **N**ation. We initially named the organization after James Madison, the father of the Constitution, to demonstrate our commitment to a government based on the original intent of the Constitution. But we are proud of our acronym as well.

In 1996 we gave nearly $350,000 to fourteen general election candidates for Congress and the Senate. Of these, four won their election, including Jim Ryun, a new home schooling parent now in Congress.

Our aim is to find one thousand people in each of the 435 congressional districts in the U.S. who will agree to contribute $10 to five different candidates for Congress. If we reach that level of membership, we will be able to give over $21 million each voting cycle to conservative challengers who meet our criteria. At a maximum, we believe there would be as many as forty such candidates each cycle. When we are at full strength, we will be able to give $500,000 to each of these forty candidates.

Home schoolers will probably continue to be a big part of this organization as it reaches its goals. I have been contacted by home schoolers in a few states who want to start an organization based on the mechanics of the Madison Project for state and local organizations. I believe that the home schooling movement will become a part, but only a part, of the most significant grassroots conservative team in this country.

This is the real way to counterbalance what the big money of the unions, businesses, and rich groupies like Emily's List do. Hundreds of thousands of people who have an organized approach to giving can more than compete with all of these other groups who have dominated politics for so long.

Madison is an example of how home schoolers are breaking out of the narrow range of political issues which are the proper subjects for home schooling organizations. (HSLDA, for example, is committed to working on issues that deal only with home schooling, education bills that touch indirectly on home schooling, parent's rights, and religious freedom.) As citizens, we are interested in a great number of additional issues that stem from our general philosophy rather from our specific convictions about family-based education.

The success and involvement of home schooling parents gives me great hope for the future of our political process and our freedom. But I am even more encouraged about the future when I see even younger home schoolers get active in the real world of political leadership.

The trends for tomorrow are clear from the present activities I see among home schooling parents and teachers.

■ Home schoolers will increase their broad-based political activity in both issue and electoral politics. We will see more and more home schooling parents and graduates elected and appointed as officials, along with many more in secondary roles as behind-the-scenes activists.

■ Home schoolers will be a significant force in driving the conservative right toward a balanced libertarian agenda, moving government away from an interventionist position, whether the goal is conservative or liberal intervention.

■ Young people who have seen the need to fight for freedom first-hand will be disproportionately involved in "public square" occupations and endeavors. A high percentage of home schoolers will become journalists, lawyers, politicians, or will be involved in other professions relating to public life. For the vast majority of home schooled children, political activism will be a lifelong interest even when they are not pursuing a public square career.

■ Home schoolers will help to move the educational choice
movement away from vouchers and toward tax credits in order
to guarantee freedom from government restriction.

■ Home schoolers will become the significant force in our society
needed to balance the children's rights movement.

■ Home schooling parents will become the model upon which
public school parents create a "parents only" organization
(kicking the T out of the PTA) and take back substantial control of public education from both the bureaucracy and the
unions. If I am wrong, public schools will continue to spiral
downward in public support until less than 50 percent of children in the country attend government-run schools.

The children and parents who have experienced a movement that
had to fight in politics and law to gain basic freedoms are the best kind
of activists. They have learned how to fight and win. They will use this
knowledge in other arenas. They understand and truly believe in the
principles of freedom because they have fought for them at a great
cost. They will never take freedom for granted. They love and believe
in our nation because they have seen that it is still possible to attain
one's dream by trust in God and hard work.

Home schoolers will become a new generation of Patrick Henrys.
They have lived under both oppression and freedom, and they love
freedom enough to fight for it valiantly.

3

Support Groups of the Future

When my wife and I first started home schooling in Olympia, Washington, we had a support group meeting whenever the only other Olympia home schooling couple came over for a visit. Shortly after we moved to Virginia, we attended our first real support group meeting, which was held in a public meeting room supplied by a local grocery store. The main thrill of the evening was that the twenty or so couples in the room were all home schooling their children!

The old days when home schoolers went to support group meetings to prove to themselves that they all—or at least most—weren't totally weird are long gone. The need for encouragement and fellowship is still a big, big reason why parents—especially moms—are drawn into support groups, but support groups do a great deal more these days.

World-Class Support in Orlando

Jim and Linda Werner were two of home education's first pioneers to envision the support group of the future. Their effort is now called

Circle Christian School, which is headquartered in sunny Orlando, Florida. Circle Christian represents over 520 families who are active members of the group, representing nearly 1,000 school-age children.

The key to Jim and Linda's vision was providing a level of professional quality services to families to relieve some of the burdens and difficulties a family encounters in home schooling. Their full-service vision is not that unusual today, but in 1985 when they founded Circle Christian, the movement was still dominated by self-sufficient pioneers who tended to frown on anyone who didn't do everything by himself—including weaving his own clothes and grinding his own flour.

Circle Christian's operation features six paid staffers, including Jim Werner, who is now the full-time administrator. It takes all of one of their staffer's time just to coordinate the field trips, since Circle Christian schedules approximately 150 field trips each year. Naturally, in the Orlando area, there is an abundance of opportunities to visit the various theme and amusement parks nearby. But, of course, these grow old easily—especially for families who are looking for a variety of educational experiences for their children.

Appreciation of the fine arts appears to be high on the agenda for many of Circle Christian's families, since the group's field trips include regular trips to the various museums in the greater Orlando area. Especially popular are the once-a-month outings to theaters with live dramatic and musical productions.

Some of the more traditional kinds of field trips—visits to the police and fire departments—are still very much a part of the litany of choices offered to Circle Christian's families.

Naturally, no family could possibly attend 150 field trips—or else the school year would offer nothing else. But, then again, who would want to go on a field trip with all the children in a group of a thousand? Support groups of the future offer such a variety of choices and dates that families can pick and choose the trip that matches their needs and interests. No matter what kind of spin a parent places on the "joy of togetherness," a seventeen-year-old has a hard time enjoying a petting zoo when accompanied by several dozen six-year-olds he sees once a month. A large, well-organized group offers the chance for some sensible grouping by age and interest on field trips.

They may have more field trips of greater variety than a busy parent could offer, but Circle Christian's main boon to its member–families is a high level of academic support.

Circle Christian offers its teaching parents courses each year that help them to become more proficient as home instructors. Recent classes included a course on learning styles and another on assisting a special needs child.

Marie Hamrick is Circle Christian's director of education who helps to coordinate a plethora of counseling,

The need for encouragement and fellowship is still a big, big reason why parents—especially moms—are drawn into support groups, but support groups do a great deal more these days.

assistance, and specialized instruction for the member–families. Marie, with the help of two assistants, offers curriculum counseling and standardized testing for all families. At the high school level, she helps parents plan specific courses for their students to ease the process of college admission. Assistance with scholarship research is also available. Circle Christian gives its graduates well-prepared high school transcripts and high school diplomas. Eight of Circle Christian's thirty graduates in 1996 qualified for the prestigious Florida Academic Scholar award—a much higher percentage of graduates than most traditional schools.

Circle Christian also offers a number of specialized and supplemental courses, particularly at the high school level. One home schooling dad with a professional background in chemistry teaches a weekly chemistry lab, while the students learn the balance of the course from a parent at home. A similar biology lab is offered, as are three language classes other than English—Spanish, French, and American Sign Language. One mom, who is a semiprofessional actress, leads a drama group, while another, who is a former physical education instructor at Ball State University, has taught a state-mandated "book course" in physical education. A journalism class published a student newspaper for the 1996–97 school year.

Circle Christian fields high school boys' varsity and junior varsity basketball teams that play on a regular Christian school league. Younger levels of children play on a variety of sports teams against traditional Christian schools.

A high school vocal ensemble performs frequently in the community, and there are high school and middle school service clubs that serve the community through groups like the Salvation Army, Give the Kids the World, and Operation Christmas Child.

A typical home schooling family will participate in only one or two of these many activities each week. The essence of a family's program is still heavily comprised of in-home instruction. But when a child has a special need or desire, quality services are available for that family in an atmosphere that fully embraces the home schooling philosophy and the parents' Christian values. Of course, these kinds of services are not free, but they are not expensive when compared to the cost of private school tuition and fees. Enrollment is $175 per year for a family, plus $200 per child, with a maximum of $775 per family.

Volunteer-Driven Support in Rochester

Many families prefer a more old-fashioned approach to support groups where volunteer parents plan a few activities for support and encouragement. Even such traditional support groups are learning to work together in a way which demonstrates innovative thinking that others will want to emulate in the future.

Hearts at Home L.E.A.H. is a support group in the Rochester, New York, area affiliated with the statewide group Loving Education at Home. Hearts at Home does not place the burden of leadership on a single mother or family, which was so often the case in the early days of home school support groups. Rather, the leadership is handled by a team of four couples who share the responsibilities and tasks of leading the group.

Brenda Foster, a member of the Hearts at Home leadership, says that their group has not felt the need to offer group classes for children who are dropped off for instruction. Instead, some creative supplemental courses meet once-a-month in an old-fashioned co-op style. The key rule for Hearts at Home's co-op classes is that every parent must attend with his or her child and every parent must take a turn in the instruction.

The company that sells the extraordinarily popular American Girl dolls has created a history program that focuses on the periods of American history represented by each of its dolls. Hearts at Home offers a mom-and-daughter co-op course using this creative material. Seventeen girls from thirteen families meet each month for this class, which brings substance and depth to a study that makes history come alive for them.

Another co-op for mothers and young children is entitled "Primary Passport." Using a curriculum developed by a home schooling mom, Jane Claire Lambert, this co-op enables "our kids to travel around the world through books," says Brenda Foster. Each month a different classic children's book, such as *Madeline, Mike Mulligan and the Steam Shovel,* or *Ping,* is the focus of a unit study on the geography and culture of the nation featured in the story. Each mom has to prepare only one unit, and her child receives an entire year of this fun and learning through shared efforts.

While the moms and young children "travel around the world," in a room in a friendly church, the older children meet down the hall for a creative writing co-op. In this case a single teacher has volunteered to present the class to older elementary children each month. Five total co-op programs are going this year at Hearts at Home for its eighty-five member–families.

Like most support groups, Hearts at Home offers a good variety of field trip opportunities. Ten major field trips are given each year, and a different family is responsible for the planning and execution of each one. Visits to the Rochester Museum and Science Center and the Rochester Planetarium, a riverboat tour of the Erie Canal, and (what would have been a big hit in my home) a tour of a toy factory were the highlights for the most recent school year.

Hearts at Home also offers an entertaining evening as an alternative to Halloween each October 31. The Harvest Party and Square Dance draws up to two hundred children, and again, no drop-offs—parents are there as well.

The monthly meetings are for parents only and feature minicourses on a number of interesting topics. The presentation, "You don't need a goat to home school," on a recent list caught my eye. I am sure that the audience had convincing proof that choosing an alternative form of education does not necessarily commit your family to a "whole grain" lifestyle in other areas of family living. More traditional offerings have included instruction on learning styles, priorities, and scheduling, and talks by both a reading specialist and a vision specialist. An especially important session is spent each year instructing families on the process of complying with New York's comprehensive home schooling regulations.

Hearts at Home sends its twelve-page newsletter to its members six times per year. The cost for membership and the newsletter is $30 a year, which includes $12 for membership in the state organization L.E.A.H.

Hearts at Home is clearly a Christian organization, but it is open to any family regardless of their own faith. "Each family wanting to join has to read our statement of faith and sign a form that says they understand it. We don't require them to agree to it, but we want them to understand what kind of atmosphere they are getting into," Brenda Foster says.

Hearts at Home has mastered the basics of old-fashioned support groups. Shared leadership and shared labor enable this group to offer a number of diverting and helpful activities without requiring one or two moms to sacrifice their own home schooling experience for the sake of the support group.

Statewide Academic Support in South Carolina

For a number of years, HSLDA fought more cases in the courtroom in South Carolina than in any other state. The home schooling law in that state was littered with provisions that made life difficult for a great number of people who asked only for freedom to educate their children responsibly. Zan Tyler, who stands five-feet-two in a stiff breeze, is a woman who simply refuses to bow to government oppression. After a number of attempts to solve the legal problems with the existing home schooling law, Zan tried an "end run" around the law using an obscure provision in South Carolina's private school statute. This provision allowed self-regulation

Many home schooling moms, especially those in their first few years, simply want close companionship with others who are embarked on a similar journey.

of private schools for schools that were members of the state association for traditional private schools "or other similar organizations."

In 1990 Zan asked me for assistance in creating a state home schooling organization that would qualify as a "similar organization" within the meaning of this law. We did our very best to implement the accountability and structure that this esteemed private school organization had used to keep the government satisfied that self-regulation was indeed all that was necessary in South Carolina. This was the birth of the South Carolina Association of Independent Home Schools (SCAIHS).

But despite our best efforts, a handful of school districts would not accept the legitimacy of a family avoiding public school regulation of their home schooling by simply joining SCAIHS. The 120 brave families that joined SCAIHS that first year ended up in court again in South Carolina. The trial judge who first heard our case ruled against the SCAIHS alternative, and I was in the process of preparing the appellate briefs when Zan took her situation to the state legislature.

Based on the credibility Zan and the other leaders of SCAIHS had earned through many years of responsibly discharging their duties as home schooling parents and leaders, the legislature was willing in 1992 to grant SCAIHS, and only SCAIHS, the right to be self-governing as a legal alternative to any form of government regulation. Zan and I both tried to get the bill written to allow other groups the same alternative, but the State Department of Education was unwilling to comply.

In 1996 our original dream of opening self-governance of home education to a variety of groups became law with the passage of a new amendment to this statute. SCAIHS had operated in a manner that had won credibility for all home schoolers.

It is my fervent hope that this new, broadened "freedom" experiment in South Carolina will serve as a precedent for providing home schoolers a self-governing alternative to government oversight in many more states.

When one examines the quality and scope of the program offered by SCAIHS, it is not hard to understand why it has been successful in winning recognition and freedom.

SCAIHS has grown from the initial 120 families to nearly 1,100 families, with almost 1,900 students. SCAIHS, under Zan's continued leadership, serves these member–families with a staff of sixteen, including twelve educational professionals. These twelve, who serve as academic advisors to the teaching parents, have the kinds of credentials the government recognizes. Three have masters degrees, seven have degrees in education, and the balance have college degrees in substantive disciplines. But, more importantly, eleven of the advisors are home schooling moms (some whose children have completed their education) and have both the heart and the experience to provide real help for those parents who choose home education.

SCAIHS offers an annual "new members" orientation course to give all families instruction on responsible home education. Also offered is a "how to home school" seminar that is open to the public.

The heart of the SCAIHS program is the academic assistance it makes available to the member–families, not on the basis of a centralized rule, but upon the needs and desires of the member–families. Since the program is open to all home schoolers throughout the state, the academic counselors will assist teaching parents either in person in the office in Columbia or by phone.

SCAIHS sells no curriculum, but will help a home schooling mom figure out which of the many offerings will be best for her children. And when a teaching mom is having a particularly horrible day—as we all do on occasion—she can call a SCAIHS academic counselor for assistance in solving either the academic or even the disciplinary problem that is at the heart of the difficulty. "A lot of children who are coming out of the public schools," Zan Tyler says, "have a hard time adjusting to the discipline of a home schooling program. We have been able to help many moms make this critical transition with their children based on a lot of collective home schooling experience with our own kids."

SCAIHS offers its 257 high school students credit units, transcripts, diplomas, SAT testing, and a full "cap and gown" graduation ceremony. High school students are also offered the opportunity to participate in Boy's State (Zan expects Girl's State to follow soon) just like the more traditional schooling programs. An annual Career Day is also offered to help home schooled students understand how they can make the transition into the adult working world.

A two-day creative writing workshop is taught for younger children, in part by the developer of the popular McGee and Me series produced by Focus on the Family.

"We spend a lot of time and resources helping families with special needs," Tyler says. "These children perhaps benefit more from home education than anyone."

Parents in South Carolina join SCAIHS—a freedom-winning support group of the future—because of the credibility, counseling, and encouragement it offers to home schooling parents. A number of parents also willingly pay an annual fee (the fee varies according to age and number of children) to have someone else take care of the administrative side of home education so that they can concentrate on teaching their children.

Marching to the Beat of a Different Drum in California

Not all support groups of the future will be broad-based, multi-issue organizations. Some will have a single activity that offers a quality intensive experience for home schooling students.

One of the pioneers of this kind of support group is the Home School Patriots, a marching Fife and Drum corps, founded in 1988 in southern California. John Eastis, a former high school band teacher, is married to Annette, a former high school drill team advisor. When they began looking for performance opportunities for their own children, it seemed only natural that they would form a home school marching band and drill team.

The Home School Patriots started with just ten children in their first year. Now they are an accomplished, award-winning marching band and drill team with over 150 students who play drums, fifes, and bells (glockenspiels, for the musical experts among us); they also twirl batons, flags, or rifles; and they have a precision drill team. The Patriots, in their red, white, and blue Minutemen outfits, have a formidable record of wins in parades and related marching band competitions. "In the past five years we have taken first or second in every competition we have entered," Annette says. "What is really amazing is that our kids practice only an hour-and-a-half each week, compared to traditional high school bands that meet each day."

The Los Angeles County Fair has made the Home School Patriots the official opening band for the fair for the past six years. And in addition to their parade schedule the band is a regular at Disneyland, Knott's Berry Farm, and a number of civic events. "The park officials are always thrilled with our students. They constantly remark about how clean-cut and well-behaved they are. We get asked back often not only because of our performance, but because the kids know how to act the whole time they are in the park," Annette told me.

John and Annette Eastis have information they are willing to share with others who would like to start similar marching groups. *Home School Patriots, PO Box 292242, Cunthelan, CA 92329-2242, (619) 868-5846.*

The Houston Home School "Tabernacle Choir"

One hundred twenty-five students from ages eight to seventeen present themselves as talented singers, polished entertainers, and a squeaky-clean, delightful sight for sore eyes in an age of nose rings and gangsta rappers. They are the Joyful Sound Home School Choir from Houston, Texas. I have seen them perform twice, and I can indeed verify they are a joy to listen to.

Paula Spencer, a former high school music teacher turned home schooling mom, created this premier musical group in 1992. The group's performance resume reads more like an accomplished college choir than a group of kids starting as young as eight and nine. They have performed for Focus on the Family's headquarters in Colorado Springs, the Houston Thanksgiving Day Parade, the Houston Ballet's Christmas Tree Lighting, and for several business organizations.

"Children's voices always appeal to people," Mrs. Spencer says. "And curiosity about home schooling has created another special point of interest for many groups. We are able to take a message into business functions that would normally not be allowed simply because of the intrigue of home schooling."

Joyful Sound's favorite program has been to go to inner-city public schools once a week for an approximately six-week period. The group's experienced singers become the music teachers and voice coaches for the inner-city students as they teach them a short selection of songs. And at the end of the time, the home school singers and their public school trainees perform a concert together for parents and the community.

It takes an intensive program of training to attain these kinds of results, but Paula Spencer has found a creative way to do this that fits in with the home school lifestyle. All practices are during the day on Tuesdays. Some of the more involved and advanced students are at practice nearly all day. Several specialty choirs and groups meet during the day; the main concert choir meets for three hours.

Some students travel as far as seventy miles to participate in the group. And there are opportunities for up to sixty performances a year. Most students participate in about thirty to forty concerts and appearances. Families are able to pick and choose the performances that fit best on their own schedule, with only a handful of required concerts during the year.

Paula Spencer says she is willing to help others learn to lead such choirs and has received inquiries from home schoolers in a few other areas. Her dream is to have a national adjudicated home school choir contest, where the competition is not against other groups but against the absolute standards of excellence.

Close Camaraderie in Colorado

Not all families want or need the bright lights of performing for their families. Many home schooling moms, especially those in their first few years, simply want close companionship with others who are embarked on a similar journey.

Many of the first-generation support groups majored in camaraderie. But many of these groups tended to burn out their leaders. Another problem in many early groups was the tension that developed when many different home schooling philosophies began to have real-life implications.

Chris and Robin Zook of Colorado Springs founded a group in 1996 that majors in close fellowship, but appears to have solved two crucial difficulties that face most smaller support groups. Their group is called FACET—Families Accountable for their Children's Education and Training.

(Incidently, I am always fascinated with the creative acronyms home schoolers can dream up for their support groups. My own suggestion, United Parent Christian Home—educators Under Christ's Kingdom, or UPCHUCK, is still available for any group wishing to adopt it. But, I digress.)

Robin Zook told me that they have adopted an organizational style suggested by Jethro to his son-in-law Moses when he was struggling with the heavy responsibilities of one man leading a very large group. FACET operates a chain of interconnected support groups, each of which is limited to a maximum of ten families. FACET had six groups of ten families in its first year of operation. They will deliberately limit the group to ten groups of ten families. After that, they will encourage others to start similar, but completely independent, groups so that the level of intimate fellowship can be maintained.

FACET offers a few activities for the entire network. There is an annual ladies retreat; a project fair for science, history, and more; a trip to the symphony; and members can participate in a local qualifying round for the National Geography Bee.

But FACET's focus is on activity within the small groups of its ten families, which tend to organize on the basis of individual needs. Two of the small groups are just for moms. Two are just for couples. The other two have a variety of meetings for moms, dads, and couples. One of the mothers' groups is organized for those with young children, and the other is for those with older kids.

Each of these groups is emphatically Christian-based, and FACET's goal is "to keep Christ in the center." This commitment to Christian principles and to the importance of small-group intimacy provides the philosophical unity that is so important in a smaller, relation-centered group. And the leadership of each of the six smaller groups meets together as a leadership team with the Zooks for encouragement and direction in advancing their mission to Christian home schooling families.

The budget of FACET is extraordinarily modest. Each of the small groups contributes just $15 total to support the cost of FACET's newsletter. When FACET is at its membership limit, its entire budget will be just $150. If only the government could learn to run programs in this fashion!

Home Schoolers Do Fair-ly Well in California

At the other end of the size spectrum is the modestly named "Home School Fair" held in Ontario, California—in the southern part of the state—which boasts the nation's largest home schooling population. The fair attracts over 1,400 exhibits from home schooled children (many children submit more than one exhibit), and nearly two thousand friends and family members turn out to see a huge visible display of home schooling excellence.

Founded in 1989, this annual one-day "support group" outing is orchestrated by a home schooling mom who claims, "I'm allergic to meetings." Donna Woodson, who also leads an independent study program for about forty home school families called the Olive Tree Christian School, as well as a support group by newsletter for over 150 families, organizes this colossal one-day event.

Students can of course submit science projects (in the categories of earth, physical, or life science) to this fair. But not everyone likes to make huge papier-mâché beetles, so this fair also features contests for history projects, writing (poetry or creative writing), baked goods, arts and crafts, and sewing. "A combination country fair and school fair," Woodson calls it.

The exhibits are judged by professionals from relevant fields, and none has home schooling connections. This independence not only keeps the contestants assured of impartiality, but it also serves to educate a great number of opinion-makers on the quality of work done by home schoolers.

As if this weren't enough for a single day, Woodson has expanded the event to include a mini-Olympics for the home schooled kids. There are races of 50, 100, and 440 yards, as well as running and standing broad jumps. There are different age categories and divisions for both boys and girls. This well-run event attracts over 500 children to compete.

More informal contests include ice cream eating, pie eating, Hula Hooping (which I might have difficulty getting around my waist after the ice cream and pie contests), and a form of competitive leap-frogging that appears to be loosely based on Mark Twain's story about a frog-jumping contest.

Home schooling families and some local support groups offer food booths and carnival-type games as fund raisers. A number of home schooling curriculum suppliers can't stay away from such a large number of home schoolers gathered in one place.

All in all, it sounds like a great day. This is just the kind of event that can bring about a real sense of community as well as achievement for home schoolers in a large area. These kinds of fairs and contests will begin to appear all over America as others seize the initiative and follow the "I hate meetings but I love fun" philosophy so brilliantly exemplified by Donna Woodson.

Dads? In a Support Group?

Bob Likes runs a unique support group in the West San Fernando Valley of southern California. HOME (Homes Organized for Meaningful Education) was founded in 1982 shortly after the initial broadcast about home education on Focus on Family. (That radio program was what first introduced my wife to home schooling and may be the best historical fix for launching the modern home schooling movement.)

Bob Likes tells me that HOME has two principles that run the group. "First is loyalty belongs to the family—loyalty to the support group is always secondary. And second, we emphasize the importance of male leadership."

Mothers have historically wanted support groups to serve as a source of encouragement for their daily activities in home education. They also have an intense desire for unwavering, tangible support from their husbands. HOME blends both of these by giving them a group in which the men are required to demonstrate their support for their wives by doing a lot of the routine work that enables the group to function.

Bob Likes makes everybody participate. "Do something or don't come," he says. "Everyone does a little."

HOME offers both Park Days and Pie Nights. Park Days are a fairly common activity for support groups in areas with good weather, where moms get together and talk while the kids play. The Pie Nights, however, require an active sacrifice from the dads. They are required to stay home with all the kids, "and no complaining," Likes says, while mom goes to a fun evening out and eats pie. It may not be a glamorous form of male leadership but it is the kind that the mothers will remember.

HOME offers a number of field trips, a drama group, a choir, and a basketball team that went to the National Home School Tournament in Colorado. These are fairly typical kinds of activities for any group. But a wife who is relieved from doing the planning because her husband has shown his true support for home schooling by doing some "grunt" work will feel quite differently about attending an activity she has not had to plan or execute. It can be a relief rather than yet another responsibility.

Bob Likes planned his first-ever dads regular seminar that took place in early 1997. Using the book, *How a Man Raises His Daughter*, by Michael Farris (Bethany House, 1996), Bob intends to encourage fathers to continue their role of servant–leaders by learning how best to raise daughters in a way that is different from the world about us. "Somehow in the midst of the feminist lie, we need to figure out how our girls can be proudly feminine." My eighteen-year-old daughter calls it being "an empowered traditionalist." But the HOME dads will learn that. It's in the book.

I strongly encourage dads to take advantage of the opportunity to prove to their wives that they really are team players in their home schooling programs by volunteering to do some of the unglamorous labor it takes to make a support group's activities a success. Lots of men are willing to volunteer to serve as emcee for meetings or give a devotional talk, but the real labor is planning, organizing, mailing, labeling, stuffing, and registering. HOME has hit a home run with the husband-involvement philosophy.

Guidelines for the Future

The future of home schooling support groups will be driven by a divergent group of needs that they are designed to fill. Some needs will be best met by highly organized, professional services created by inventive home schooling entrepreneurs. Others will find their greatest support from small, homey, volunteer-led groups that emphasize fellowship and encouragement. The need that is to be fulfilled will dictate the form of the future support.

But all support groups need to take to heart a central principle in their collective thinking: *home schooling moms are being pushed to the limit and need assistance and relief.* Groups that place too great a burden on wives will wither away to nothing. Groups that give moms a sense that a little effort on their part yields a great result for their children and families will be wildly successful.

My thinking about guidelines for the future is best organized around the various needs that mothers have.

Administrative assistance. In a great many states, the legal structure requires moms to keep detailed and comprehensive records. Other states have no such legal requirements, and record-keeping *for elementary and middle school students* is a matter of personal preference. But no matter where one lives, record-keeping is truly essential for high school students. This is primarily true for college admissions purposes, but it can also be a pragmatic necessity for entering the military or any number of other adult opportunities, including some jobs.

Many families will want the professionalism and structure offered by programs like Circle Christian School in Orlando, or by the South Carolina Association of Independent Home Schools. In California, independent study programs like Keystone Academy in Norwalk, which offer formal high school academic planning and counseling, transcripts, testing, and diplomas, are nearly universal among home schoolers.

The Florida, South Carolina, and California support services all sprang up because of the legal climate in those states. But services survive and are expanding—especially at the high school level—even after the legal crises have passed, because many parents recognize the value of administrative services.

Professional administrative services will be among the support groups of the future because they pass the number one rule—they relieve busy mothers of unnecessary details so they can concentrate on teaching and loving their children.

Academic counseling. Someone could have made a lot of money off my wife Vickie when she was teaching math to my daughter, Katie, by answering her questions using Saxon's Advanced Mathematics book. Vickie, on the other hand, has since served as a volunteer "academic counselor" on an informal basis to a number of new home schooling moms who were nervous about the basics.

Future academic counseling services will be of two varieties— one professional and one volunteer—and will track pretty closely with my own family's experience.

Donna Woodson, who organizes the Home School Fair in California, has found the key to the volunteer kind of academic counseling. Every experienced home schooling family is asked to volunteer to be a "coach" for a brand new family in the support group. In this way every family that needs help has someone to turn to, but no family (and particularly the leader) is overburdened with constant phone calls for assistance.

No professional educator, no matter how clever or well intentioned, can ever serve as home schooling coach for all those first- and second-year jitters like a mom who has been there and done it.

But as our movement begins to have more and more high school level students as part of the mix, the need for course-specific academic counseling will intensify. It is in this area that professional services—both locally operated, phone-based counseling, and even online academic counseling—will continue to flourish and succeed.

Mothers who have genuine academic expertise as well as home schooling experience will be in great demand. Those who have graduated their last child after ten years of home schooling really need to be looking into the business aspect of home education counseling. Home schooling experience plus genuine academic expertise is what has catapulted SCAIHS and Circle Christian School into major operations with a good number of employees.

Another group of likely academic counseling entrepreneurs are young men and women who have recently graduated from home schooling and are willing to assist both parents and students with their academic questions on matters within the graduate's expertise.

An area of highly specialized academic counseling will be for those who have children with special needs. The HSLDA has for many years employed a person with the full-time responsibility of assisting our member families who have children with special needs. Our counselor helps families find a qualified individual who truly understands a child's particular disability to serve as a coach for the parent.

Another leading organization for these kinds of families is NATH-HAN—the **NAT**ional c**H**allenged **H**omeschoolers **A**ssociated **N**etwork. NATHHAN has a support network of around seven thousand individuals, comprised mainly of families. Some of these are home schooling professionals willing to help, some are companies with an interest in serving disabled home schoolers, while most are families who teach special needs children at home. NATHHAN's greatest contribution is maintaining a tremendous referral network of both consulting professionals and experienced home schooling parents who can help others meet these special needs. In addition to a quarterly newsletter, Tom and Sherry Bushnell, who lead the organization, also publish a family directory, maintain a lending library, and speak regularly at home schooling fairs and conferences.

The bigger local support programs like those described in this chapter will also be an important, local source of help for those who desire to home school their special needs child.

Socialization. Every home schooler would be rich if a $1 fee were imposed on those who ask, "What about socialization?"

Children do need opportunities to interact with a variety of different people, including, but certainly not limited to, children their own age. But it is neither desirable nor efficient to mix socialization activities with academic instruction. All parents want their children to "concentrate" on their studies. Somehow they seem surprised when their children have trouble concentrating on academics in a room full of thirty kids who are committed to partying on a moment's notice.

Socialization opportunities for home schooling students will be most apparent when mixed with a traditional extracurricular activity. Sports teams just for home schoolers that compete in regular school leagues will become more and more common—particularly in states where public school officials like to tweak the noses of our families by denying access to public school athletics. (Incidently, this is a problem that is best solved politically. Lawsuits in this area are difficult.) Choirs like Joyful Sound and bands like the Home School Patriots will begin to penetrate even midsize to smaller regions as the numbers of home schoolers continue to expand rapidly.

As was mentioned in Chapter 1, I believe that debate and forensics teams will also be a vital part of the future of home education. In addition to the rhetorical training, these kinds of speech clubs can provide a wholesome method of interaction for young people. When young people have a purpose, interaction can be quite positive. When they are just hanging out, look out.

Service clubs will also be important. I really like the idea of a Tutoring Club, which would take older, successful home schooling students into the center city to give hope to those—usually younger kids in elementary school—who are trapped by the failure of urban public education. I know of no such club, but it seems like something that an inner-city church would be more than happy to help bring to their community.

I am amazed at the creativity and scope of the field trips that are offered to younger home schooled children (as well as their older brothers and sisters). These great outings mix socialization and educational benefits for everyone. So long as standards of behavior are enforced, these are also a good advertisement to the general public for home schooling.

Fellowship. Every home schooling mom needs a friend who also home schools. Every home schooling dad needs a friend who will hold him accountable for carrying out his responsibility to his family in this arena of life.

The first-generation support groups were formed primarily for this purpose. It will always remain a need. I believe that the small group which is clustered by both geography and age of children will be the most successful fellowship groups in the long run. FACET in Colorado Springs provides an interesting model.

Bob Likes of HOME told me, "When we were small, every parent was an aunt and uncle to every child in the group. It was very special. And it is something that we have lost in part as we have grown larger."

Small compatible fellowship groups, linked with more groups to do other things, will always be the backbone of the home school support groups of the future.

4

High-Tech Learning

A missionary walks through the jungles of New Guinea, describing the plants, animals, and topography to a group of excited students who accompany him. One student asks the missionary to turn over a fallen log. He wants to see if the insects are different from those in Wisconsin. Suddenly, a group of aboriginal hunters appear in a clearing ahead. The missionary has seen these men before, but it is the first glimpse for the students. The aborigines are reputedly dangerous when they see total strangers. But the students are in no danger whatsoever because their tour is being conducted via a "point of view" camera attached to the missionary's hat, which transmits to a satellite feed, which sends a video transmission live over the Internet straight into the students' homes. The students ask questions via microphones attached to their computers; this allows for "real time" communication.

The technology to implement such a high-tech geography lesson exists today. It is still extremely expensive. But in just a few years, the devices will likely cost no more than a camcorder and a cellular phone.

High-tech educational hardware and software offer the prospect of revolutionizing education. "If teachers are freed from reinventing instruction, freedom from always being the content person and the dispenser of information, they will have more time for one-to-one contact with learners." So says Don Smellie, head of the Department of Instructional Technology at Utah State. His comments praising the prospect of one-to-one contact in public schools have a definite ring of familiarity to home schoolers. "The idea of putting thirty-five young people in a box and only giving the teacher a textbook and a piece of chalk, and expecting positive results, is ludicrous," Smellie says.

The most convincing piece of evidence I discovered about the radical change that technology offers for home education appeared in an ad in *Home School Computing* magazine (now a section of *The Teaching Home* magazine). "Brighten Your Future... Earn High School Credit with HOMER," the ad proclaimed. A computer-based course offering instruction in Business Education, English, Mathematics, Science, Social Studies, and Vocational Education is available through none other than the North Dakota Department of Public Instruction. I really couldn't believe my eyes. This is the same department that waged a bitter war on home schoolers throughout the 1980s and caused me to appear personally before the supreme court of North Dakota on numerous occasions. To have this department go from being one of the worst enemies of home education in the entire country, to selling computer-based instruction to home schoolers throughout the entire country, is an absolutely amazing turnaround.

Technology can be of great assistance to home schooling parents and children, but no one should think that a child's complete education can be offered through a computer or a satellite dish. Great education of the future will be both high-tech and high-touch, as John Naisbitt predicted in 1982 in the runaway bestseller *Megatrends*. Home schooling succeeds in large part because it offers the greatest form of high-touch education available. It is well recognized that home schooling parents offer far greater individual interaction with their children than is humanly possible in the institutional classroom setting.

Technology can have a dehumanizing effect on any form of instruction. No one believes that multiple hours in front of a television set

The Dangers of the Web

A missionary tramping through a dangerous jungle presents an appropriate illustration for another aspect of high-tech learning, because, like the jungle, danger lurks around every corner.

As I was researching this chapter, I spent some time on the Internet looking at a number of current research tools and services. On a home schooling bulletin board I saw a reference to a program which offered free foreign language instruction in three or four languages. I dutifully wrote down the World Wide Web address for this service and tried to find it through a Web search engine. I probably didn't know how to do the search correctly, but I got a result listing twenty-five sites for me to look at. The first site on the list was a major listing of a whole group of Web pages for those practicing witchcraft. A little further down the list was another advertising blatant pornography.

High-tech learning is definitely going to be a major factor in education. But certain aspects of this technology are full of the danger that children—looking for help in learning Spanish, for example—will fall in with witches, pornographers, and child molesters.

The good news is that a number of products are being offered which claim to be able to "filter" the Internet so that no pornography reaches your home computer. It remains to be seen whether these filters will work effectively to screen out other forms of offensive materials as well, such as the witchcraft Web site I accidently found. One of my most high-tech friends tells me that MIT is working on a new variation of an Internet rating system that may solve the problem completely. This rating system will allow independent groups to attach their "affirmative rating" to any site on the Web. A family's home computer would then be programmed to allow only those sites bearing their favorite "seals of approval" into their home.

offers a good means of increasing either educational skills or the ability to interact with other people. By the same token, a child who spends six hours a day in front of a computer screen with no live human interaction will be similarly stunted in both academic and human terms.

Two factors will make educational technology primarily a positive influence as it is applied to home education. First, as we shall see in greater detail in just a moment, the technology of the future will permit much greater human interaction than has been possible heretofore. And second, home school parents will not use technology for the bulk of their children's lessons. A great part of the desire to home school involves the heartfelt conviction that a parent needs personally to influence a child's life through intensive interaction. Accordingly, parents will always want to provide as much of their child's educational experience as they possibly can.

A number of home schooling parents recognize that educational technology will be used to fill in the gaps in their programs. At the elementary level, technology will be used primarily to accomplish two important things.

First, computer technology can relieve a home schooling mom from a number of routine tasks that are just as well done on a machine. Memorization of basic math facts can be done with computerized flash cards in a way that a child will enjoy, and more importantly, will relieve mom from a time-consuming routine task. Spelling drills, including weekly spelling tests, can be done on a computer and, again, mom is relieved from routine and can concentrate on matters requiring more skill in instruction.

A second way that technology will be used at the elementary level is for educational enrichment. Foreign languages, both modern and ancient, should be learned as early as possible. And most home schooling parents recognize that technology is the only realistic way for their child to begin mastering them. History and geography lessons are another form of enrichment from this technology. The ability to see another land, including historical sites, can often make history come alive. When I took my oldest daughter to Versailles she understood how easy it would be for the French revolutionaries to condemn the gaudy excesses of the regime that it toppled. Technology will soon allow all parents—even those without Frequent Flyer awards—to take their child on a tour of Versailles.

High-Tech High

Educational technology will in the future play an even greater role in secondary education in home schooling. Many parents are reluctant to home school their high school students—or do it believing that the character qualities gained outweigh the technical academic skills lost. As technology becomes more affordable and as more appropriate content is offered, parents will not have to make choices between first-class character and a first-class technical education. The vast majority of home schooling parents will use educational technology primarily in the areas of advanced math, science, and foreign language instruction—in other words, the courses which are considered to be the most challenging for many parents. This is not to say that there will not be a number of other specialized and advanced classes made available in a wide variety of disciplines. In fact, as a result of my work on this book, I am offering a course in constitutional law over the Internet through Escondido Tutorial Services. Many other home schooling parents and other friendly folk with high levels of expertise can be expected to follow suit with specialized courses that appeal to at least some segment of the home schooling community.

"Home schooling children of the future will have the ability to go into a chemistry laboratory and participate in experiments even with materials that would be expensive and otherwise considered dangerous," says Mary Pride, author and publisher of *Practical Home Schooling* and one of the home schooling movement's most technologically advanced advocates. "A student will be able to interact with a lab scientist and suggest different alternatives and watch the results live on their computer screen," she says.

Some forms of high-tech learning will simply be to offer online assistance when a high school student gets stuck and the parent is unable to figure out the answer. I know that my wife and I would have happily signed up for an online service that answered questions about Saxon's Advanced Mathematics course last year. About three times a week we got stumped on a problem that took us anywhere from forty-five minutes to an hour to solve. The ability to log in to an answer service, e-mail our question, and get the answer back in a few hours would have been most welcome.

Other parents will take advantage of complete advanced math courses which can be offered either on a computer disk or via an online tutorial. "If anything can be taught well on a computer it should be mathematics," says Scott Somerville, who was a computer programmer before going to Harvard Law School. Somerville, who now works with me at the HSLDA, has published many articles on technological issues in home education.

"Home school students' math scores in the upper levels are higher than public school students—but the differential is much less than both math scores in the earlier grades and verbal scores in high school," Somerville says. "Technology will be one way that home schoolers will be able to continue their strong superiority in early math scores all the way through the end of high school."

So far, most computer math products on the market that I have either purchased for my own children or have seen demonstrated are simply computer games with a math problem added from time-to-time. The "game problem" is even more exacerbated in other areas of study. "Home schoolers are looking for real educational tools," Somerville says, "not vitamin-enriched games like Carmen SanDiego which offer an educational value that is minimal at best."

Home schoolers looking for educational technology have two major sources of information that offer a great wealth of information and guidance. Mary Pride's vast wealth of materials are chock-full of information on high-tech programs and products. Her new *Big Book of Home Learning* (Crossway, 1996) will not only be available in print, but on a CD-ROM as well. Parents who wish to view various home schooling products can use the CD-ROM drive to look not only at the front covers of books, but also at a few sample pages of many of the texts the *Big Book* reviews. Moreover, through the wonders of this technology, a parent can review film clips from a number of video course presentations.

Pride also offers a great variety of information and material in the online environment of the World Wide Web. Pride's home page can be found at www.home-school.com. She also offers a forum on America Online.

Pride's *Practical Home Schooling* magazine intends to offer online lesson plans for free in the future. For example, a lesson plan in Art History could be offered with links to Web sites offered by the Louvre and other major museums.

Another source for parents looking for educational technology information is *Home School Computing*—a section of *The Teaching Home* magazine, a highly recommended resource for the home schooler. Farren Constable, author of *Home School Computing*, believes that while there is a great future for technical assistance for home schooling, there is a long way to go before the course offerings reach their full potential. "I'm not impressed at all with most products

> **Technology will be one way that home schoolers will be able to continue their strong superiority in early math scores all the way through the end of high school.**

claiming to be a complete curriculum on a computer," Constable says, "but there are individual course offerings which are fantastic."

One of Constable's favorites is a computer course in foreign language instruction offered by Syracuse Language Systems called *Triple Play Plus*. The genius of this system is that the student not only sees the words in print and hears the words correctly pronounced by a native speaker, but also the child's own voice can be recognized by the computer (via a microphone) and analyzed for correct pronunciation.

Triple Play Plus offers basic instruction in seven languages, one of which is English. The others are French, Italian, Japanese, Spanish, German, and Hebrew. It sells for $99.95 direct from the company, but can be purchased for about 40 percent less through a number of retail outlets. If you call the company's 800 number, given at the end of the chapter, they will direct you to a retail outlet near you. This price includes the microphone necessary for the computer to recognize the student's voice.

Syracuse Language Systems also offers two other forms of high-tech foreign language instruction. A multimedia program for CD-ROM called *Your Way 2.0* is available in French and Spanish. Other languages are coming. It offers all of the same speaking, hearing, and seeing skills as in *Triple Play Plus*, but both the language skills and the technology go to higher levels. Even more significantly, *Your Way 2.0* is integrated with an Internet instructional program called *Language Connect University*. It offers the opportunity for online instruction in Spanish (French is coming this year), which allows you to send recordings of your own voice to the instructor for analysis and comment.

Another program on the Internet that offers free introductory instruction in several languages is called *International Language Development*. The internet address is www.ild.com.

These programs show the shape of things to come through technology. All that is missing for the most advanced instruction is live speech between the student and the teacher. These programs seem to offer good alternatives for today, and the promise of even greater ability to learn foreign language at home in the future. And, of course, there is no reason that this technology cannot be used to offer instruction in a great variety of secondary subjects.

It seems somewhat ironic that the most advanced technology for instruction to study classical education that I have discovered is offered by our friend Fritz Hinrichs at Escondido Tutorial Services (ETS).

Hinrichs, who offers instruction in Greek and mathematics, as well as the humanities, began his long-distance learning program with ordinary teleconferencing. While he still offers this option, ETS's fastest growing group is among students who are linked by the Internet. Appearing on the students' computer screens are the words, symbols, and numbers as Hinrichs writes on an electronic whiteboard in his San Diego County headquarters. They see him work the geometry problem or write the correct sentence in Greek live on their screens.

His teaching presentation is heard live, like a radio broadcast, from the speakers in their computers. And like a live radio talk show, the students have the opportunity to interact live as well. They can type their questions or answers into their computer, and Hinrichs reads their response a few seconds later on his own computer screen. A student also has the option of calling in (assuming the family has one phone line for the computer and another for the telephone) and participating in the class discussion live by voice. When one student calls in, all the other students in the class can hear the conversation, again, just like live talk radio.

Hinrichs has the software in place to take the interaction to an even higher level. With the addition of an ISDN phone line (total cost about $50 per month, including a specialized Internet provider), the students can simply speak into their microphones, and all students in the link-up can hear each other as well as the instructor. With the ISDN lines in place, a student is one relatively small purchase away from live video interaction. With the addition of a small video camera that clips to the top of the computer, a student's face can appear live on camera in the class discussion. These cameras cost a mere $99 for a black-and-white model, and $199 for color. Every student's face would appear in a proportionately sized box on the screen, much like the beginning of the Brady Bunch television program of the 1970s. When a number of students have this modest level of new technology, students can hear and see the teacher, hear and see each other, and see hand-written material, such as math problems, live on their computer screen. In other words, they can do anything that is done in a normal classroom except peek at another student's test or shake hands at the end of class.

The Technological Options

There are three basic kinds of technology that will be employed in a variety of ways to meet educational needs of home schooling students. My own terminology for these three variants are "computer education," "broadcast education," and "online education."

Computer education refers to programs that can be purchased off-the-shelf for a certain course of instruction. The student simply puts the diskette or CD-ROM into his computer and follows the path set out for him by the instructor–programmers. CD-ROM will be the dominant force in this kind of technology for a season because it offers such a vast improvement in memory-size and visual capabilities over ordinary diskettes. Multimedia presentations will get better and better, both in academic content and in the visual skill with which it is presented.

But, if you can believe this, a newer, better technology is just around the corner and it promises to replace CD-ROMs. It is called DVD, digital video disk, and it can contain many times more information than CD-ROMs. DVDs can contain full-length motion pictures and are recordable and erasable. Farren Constable of *Home School Computing* predicts that DVDs may do away with hard drives in computers. A family's photographs will be stored on DVDs and printed on cheap color jet printers. On a recent flight I sat

> **It is not too much to believe that 40 percent of all children will receive at least some material portion of their education at home in the next ten to twenty years.**

next to the plant manager of Hewlett Packard's Color Jet Printers. The samples he showed me from a printer costing around $300 rivaled the best photofinisher I have ever seen. Instead of saving to a videotape, camcorders will to a DVD disk that can store hours and hours of home video footage.

Full encyclopedias and huge volumes of reference materials can already be stored on CD-ROM disks. For example, I have a disk that retails for around $29 which has over three thousand original works of American history including all the debates of the Constitutional Convention of 1789, the complete Federalist Papers, the Inaugural Speeches of the presidents, both volumes of *Democracy in America* by Alexis de Tocqueville, the six-volume *History of the United States* by George Bancroft, and a couple thousand other books and documents.

The research power of such a disk became clear to me during a traffic-paralyzing blizzard in early 1996. I was in the midst of hurriedly finishing a brief for Michael New, the young home schooled American soldier who was court-martialed by the Clinton administration for refusing to wear a UN uniform. We had argued in our opening brief that Article I Sec. 9 of the Constitution banned such participation in foreign armies by U.S. soldiers. The response from the secretaries of defense and army was that this provision had been rarely used and its meaning was uncertain. In less than five minutes, I was able to find and read every reference to Article I Sec. 9 in the Constitutional Convention and Federalist Papers and found a terrific quotation which gave tremendous assistance in proving the meaning of the provision according to original intent.

That kind of research would have been impossible in the past, given the time constraints we were under. It would have taken days, if not weeks, to find such a factual nugget in a mountain of original documents if we had tried to skim through the material the conventional way.

Our twelve- to eighteen-year-old students can master research skills better and faster than experienced professionals when they use the tools and resources that are available on CD-ROM and coming on DVD.

Computer education will be the best among high-tech ways to learn spelling words, math facts, state capitals, and many other things that require routine memorization. And with the kind of advanced features that *Triple Play Plus* offers in foreign language instruction, the inventiveness of the market may be the only real limit.

Computer education will also be a fabulous resource for research as whole libraries of great works get reduced to a thin silver disk that costs under $30.

Broadcast education is an alternative that people discuss with me regularly. I have had two groups of very influential Christian leaders approach me for advice about starting substantial schools that will offer full instruction in kindergarten through twelfth grade through Direct Broadcast Satellites (DBSs). DBS systems allow for eight to twelve channels to be compressed into the space that was formerly occupied by a single television channel. Companies with licenses for eight of the single channels now have the space to transmit up to ninety-six television programs simultaneously. Consequently, the opportunity to broadcast educational programs is greatly enhanced at a substantially reduced cost.

However, if all that is broadcast is a traditional teacher in a traditional classroom, the appeal to home schoolers will be limited. Why would you want to study French from a teacher in a classroom with thirty students who can barely speak the language, when you can have a live transmission from Paris and interaction with people on the street, or a teacher who interacts with you personally via the kind of technology that Fritz Hinrichs is pioneering?

DBS education has tremendous potential if the owners of this technology can learn to offer what Mary Pride calls "a dynamic interesting teacher, who presents course work in a highly visual manner." Those who have watched the video series by Francis Schaeffer, "How Shall We Then Live?" get a glimpse at what is possible.

Broadcast education will succeed only for course work where hundreds or thousands of students are attracted by a world-class instructor who knows how to present high-quality material in an interesting manner. Who wouldn't be interested in watching a show featuring David Barton teaching American history or Larry Burkett giving instruction in economics?

World-class presentations like the famous PBS series on the Civil War can be brought to life this way as well, without the necessity of a famous teacher.

Online education promises the greatest opportunities both for instruction and research. The Library of Congress has just announced a massive program to put much of its vast archives onto a Web site accessible to all. Hopefully, the library will not apply excessive political correctness to the volumes it chooses to put on line.

Much of what is online today is quite superficial. Few Web sites offer much more than some bells, whistles, and pictures. But as people learn how to make money when other people access their sites, the depth and quality of material will escalate at a pace hitherto unimaginable.

Just think of my one example of being able to search three thousand works for the Michael New case. And now instead of searching three thousand volumes, the online machinery allows you to search three hundred million documents or more.

The kind of online instruction that Escondido Tutorial Services offers and plans in the future will offer high-quality instruction available to small groups at affordable rates. It will be high tech and high touch. And the results, for the home education movement, will be staggering.

The Impact of High-Tech Education on Education Reform

High-tech education will never replace mom as a home school instructor. Hers is a job with 100 percent job security. Public school teachers who specialize in group instruction will be more challenged. If they learn to offer the kind of individualization and high specialization that will be available at home, they will survive. But as long as public educational reform is bogged down with grandiose plans of centralization à la Goals 2000 and Outcome Based Education, home schooling will continue to grow unchallenged as the dominant educational force of the future.

I used to believe that I would live to see home education represent only 5 percent to 7 percent of all school-aged children. With the prospects I now see available from high-tech education, I withdraw that prediction as being much too low. With the simultaneous advent of homebound office workers who link to a central site via computer, I believe that home schooling has a nearly unlimited potential. It is not too much to believe that 40 percent of all children will receive at least some material portion of their education at home in the next ten to twenty years. Having been directly involved in the battles for educational reform, I firmly believe that public schools will continue to operate under the institutional philosophy that will make such a percentage possible. If they would wisely reject centralization, if they would throw off the shackles of federal bureaucracy, state bureaucracy, and the teachers' unions, the parents, teachers, and principals left would have a chance of implementing many of these ideas in the public schools. But I am confident that the education establishment will be no smarter than the railroads in the early part of the twentieth century. Airlines and trucking could never really compete with railroads—or so they thought. The railroads forgot they were in the people and freight transportation business, believing that their jobs were simply to run a railroad. In the same fashion, the public education system has ceased to be about learning and is now operated for the benefit of the system and its countless employees.

A new system is coming—one that cares nothing for systems except as they deliver the needed education to children. If they work, fine; if not, new alternatives will be found. The cumbersome political mammoth that controls our nation's public schools will be unable to move and adapt to such speed and retail-oriented education. The public education ice age is coming. Public school mammoths will be frozen in place. No vote in any legislative body will be taken to do away with public schools—people will simply stop sending their children. Those who want excellence for their children will come home for school.

5

Home School–Friendly Churches

I n the early years of home schooling, few were surprised when the public education establishment reacted with severity, and on occasion outright persecution, to a family that wished to teach its own children. It was far more surprising to find this same reaction within conservative churches.

A 1996 survey found that 83.8 percent of fathers and 86.1 percent of mothers profess to be born-again Christians. The denominational background of home schoolers varies widely. The five largest denominational groups are Independent Fundamental (23.7 percent), Baptist (19.2 percent), Independent Charismatic (9.1 percent), Roman Catholic (4.8 percent), and Assembly of God (4.5 percent).[1] But there are also a fair number of so-called mainline Protestant denominations and a mixed variety of other religious groups including Jewish, Muslim, Buddhist, Latter-Day Saints, Jehovah's Witness, and New Age home schoolers. There are, of course, even a few home schoolers who say they are atheists.

I have had the privilege of defending at least one family from each of

---

[1] These are the figures for home schooling mothers.

the religious groups mentioned. From my experience, it is clear that many home schoolers who are religious people are home schooling for essentially secular reasons, such as academic, psychological, or safety concerns. But for the overwhelming majority, the decision to home school is the result of a religious conviction about Christian education and the role that God would have them play, as parents, in the lives of their children. These convictions are derived, again in the vast majority of families, from their reading and desire to adhere to the Word of God.

Thus for the huge majority of home schoolers the decision to home school rests on the same foundation as the decision to become a faithful part of a local church. Both church and home schooling are central to their lives. That is why conflict between a home educating family and its church is so traumatic. They are being torn between two of the most important facets of their lives.

In the 1980s home schoolers were looking for only minimal acceptance from their churches. In some churches where public school attendance was the norm, home schoolers were subject to ridicule and many suggestions that they were failing in their Christian duty to be "salt and light" in their public schools. And in some churches which operated their own Christian schools, home schoolers were berated for failing to support an important ministry of the local church. A number of churches, of course, were tolerant of the home schoolers and looked upon them with a live-and-let-live philosophy.

But as the years passed two significant things transpired. First, many home schoolers became far more demanding. And second, many churches decided that it was in the church's best interest to become overtly "home school friendly."

There is no doubt that many, many home schooling parents are strong-willed people. By virtue of their experience in bucking the public education establishment, home schoolers have developed a greater boldness in challenging other authority figures who act contrary to the family's convictions concerning education and child rearing. And many of the arguments they have heard and used to justify their decision vis-à-vis a public school seem to bring many church practices into serious question.

Home schoolers have come to question "age segregation." Children who are cordoned off into "age-based herds" develop peer dependency, which makes a child give greater weight to the values of his friends than to those of his parents. The evidence, both scientific and anecdotal, has proved this point in the context of institutional education. Many home schoolers ask: If age segregation is bad in public schools, why is it good in the church?

Just as age segregation is seen as a negative value, family unity is seen as a positive value. And yet, when a family exits its car at the church parking lot, family unity is often over for the balance of the day. Children and parents are scattered all over massive buildings and rarely see each other—especially if the children are young. Many parents, of course, are relieved to have other people take care of their children so that they can learn and concentrate on the spiritual teaching, but a number of home schoolers feel a

> **Yes, home schoolers are demanding that churches practice on Sunday what they preach at home Monday through Saturday.**

deep uneasiness and sense of hypocrisy when they "drop their kids off" at church. Family unity, they believe, should be both practiced and preached at church.

Most home schoolers also have strong convictions about the amount of exposure their children and teenagers have to worldly activities. This concern applies with special force to certain forms of music, as well as some forms of entertainment. But chief among home schoolers' beliefs about "worldliness" is their strong conviction that dating is unacceptable.

Dating follows the "I love you until" rule. I love you until I go off to college. Or, I love you until someone cuter comes along. Or, I love you until I get tired of you. Romance, home schoolers point out, is only of three kinds in the Bible. There is good and proper romance within marriage. And there are instances of romantic love as it develops in the hearts of people in preparation for marriage. All other instances of romantic love in the Bible are sinful examples of fornication and adultery. Home schoolers teach that sexual abstinence should not be merely physical, there should be emotional abstinence as well. After all, didn't Jesus teach us that when one commits a sinful sexual act in his heart, the sin has been committed? Dating openly encourages emotional sexual sins, which is the nearly predictable result of emotional love and physical dabbling.

When home schoolers hear this kind of teaching on Friday and Saturday at their local home school conference, there is great cognitive dissonance when on Sunday they attend a church youth group which not only tolerates dating, but considers it the norm. And they may even be ridiculed for refusing to date, even if the family is willing to tolerate the generalized atmosphere.

Yes, home schoolers are demanding that churches practice on Sunday what they preach at home Monday through Saturday. There is little doubt that many home schoolers can be quite obnoxious when they present these issues to their church's leadership. One pastor told me that when he was considering home schooling for his own family, other pastors cautioned him, saying that home schoolers were notoriously independent and unsupportive of their churches and church leaders.

Home schoolers undoubtedly embrace a religiously based philosophy which, when applied with unbending vigor, can challenge and even disrupt the traditional church practices—Sunday School, junior church, and youth group. One excellent pastor whom I know recognized the conflict, and without the slightest degree of bitterness, concluded that he didn't really want home schoolers in his church. The conflicts of philosophy were too great, and he felt that everyone would be better off if home schoolers sought fellowship with a congregation whose philosophy was closer to their own.

And this is what is beginning to happen. At first, only a few churches numbered home schooling families as a significant portion of the congregation. Now several hundred churches, including some very large ones, are predominantly home schooling in character. Far more churches, however, have decided to become home schooling friendly without being overcome by home schoolers. Lee Forstrom is the longtime senior pastor of Westwood Baptist Church in Olympia, Washington. For over a decade Lee and his wife Cheryl taught their two children, Mark and Julie, at home. Both have recently graduated and are attending Christian colleges.

Westwood is a relatively large church with over 1,300 people in regular attendance. For many years, Lee and Cheryl were among just a tiny handful of home schoolers in their congregation. Lee's philosophy has been to not be didactic about home schooling from the pulpit. He teaches biblical principles of parenting without hesitation, but leaves the specific application of home schooling to each parent's individual conscience. "The greatest sermon the home schoolers in our church preach is the quality of our children's lives," Lee says. And now there are about thirty families in the church who have begun to home school, partly because of Lee and Cheryl's example, and partly because of other factors.

One of these factors was Westwood's decision to become a home school–friendly church. Every Tuesday morning, like tens of thousands of churches in America, Westwood has a ladies' Bible study. And like most of these studies, Westwood provides a nursery for babies and preschool children. But Westwood has gone one step further; it provides a home schooling class for school-aged children, wherein the Bible is taught by a home schooling mom. Perhaps even more significantly, while offering a full range of traditional Sunday School classes, Westwood also offers a family-integrated class where parents and children meet together on Sunday mornings.

This intergenerational Sunday School and the home schooling class on Tuesdays has helped to attract some families of real quality to Westwood, Forstrom says. This blended approach allows people with differing views of child-rearing to worship peacefully together.

Grace Bible Fellowship in Walpole, New Hampshire, is a church where nearly all families with school-aged children home school. John Thompson, the teaching elder of Grace, preaches openly that the Bible directs parents to take full responsibility for the rearing of their children. But this is just "one of the venues" in which Grace Fellowship tries to integrate the Bible's instruction about parents and children into their lives, Thompson says.

One family which was drawn to Grace had been involved in a

nearby church where their teenaged daughters began to develop real conflicts with both the Christian school and the church youth group. The family believed that their daughters should not be involved in dating but should practice what home schoolers sometimes call courtship or betrothal. The two girls became tired of the teasing and pressure from their peers in the other church and started attending Grace before their parents. Soon, the whole family became part of the church under Thompson's leadership because they found a place where the family's values were shared in both teaching and practice.

"A number of families have real problems with children in Sunday Schools and youth groups who attend public schools," Thompson says. "It is not the mere fact that their parents have chosen the public school that creates the problem. The conflicts arise because the children have adopted and accepted the unbiblical values that they have found there from other students and sometimes from the official class instruction. When their children are constantly exposed to such behavior and values, they see negative consequences in the attitudes and behaviors they have worked so diligently to maintain at home."

All parents are home educators; some home school.

Grace Bible Fellowship practices family integration in all of its ministries. It now serves about twenty-five families, with attendance of about one hundred, which is a fairly typical size for an evangelical church in rural New England.

A church in Florida defied all conventional wisdom about growth by doing away with church-based Sunday School. And as a result of a new family-intensive philosophy, it has seen the church increase nearly 700 percent in size.

Pastor Bob Roach began his journey as a result of a decision of the local authorities to require his daughter to be gone from home far longer than was traditionally the practice—including many hours on a school bus each day. Sensing that he needed to seek educational alternatives, Pastor Roach and his wife began investigating home schooling. As they studied a number of books and materials, they became convinced that Deuteronomy 6 required them as parents to teach their own child.

Not too long afterward, his church, Calvary Worship Center, in Port St. Lucie, Florida, began to experience a number of difficulties due to the implementation of their traditional Sunday School program. "It suddenly occurred to me," Pastor Roach said, "that if parents are commanded to teach academic truth to their children by this passage in the Bible, then they are also required to teach them spiritual truth." Accordingly, Sunday School went home.

Pastor Roach and his staff now prepare Family Altar lessons for approximately 350 families in their own church (not to mention several other churches that are now using the material). The Family Altar program is designed to give both guidance and practical help to fathers to execute their duties as the spiritual leaders of their homes.

Other changes followed. Although the church operates a nursery, they make it quite clear that anyone who wants to keep their little ones with them in church is welcome to do so. The church also operates a nursing mothers room. Moreover, traditional Junior Church has been banished as well. Instead, families keep their three- to five-year-old children with them during singing and worship for the first half of the service. At that point an optional program for preschoolers is offered, but again families are encouraged to keep their little ones in church with them if they desire.

"In the first month after doing away with Junior Church, we had twenty-eight children come forward and accept Christ as their Savior," Pastor Roach says. It is amazing that while Junior Church was an attempt to make church relevant to young children, the adult church was actually far more effective in reaching these children for salvation.

Not all of Calvary Worship Center's members are home schoolers. Only about 10 percent of the church's families are now engaged in home education. But the church correctly sees that, from a spiritual perspective, the issue is getting parents to lead their children's spiritual lives at home.

A man who shares this perspective is Eric Wallace. Eric heads a two-pronged ministry to families from his base in Springfield,

Virginia. The governing philosophy of Eric's work is: *All parents are home educators; some home school.* With this open attitude, it is easy to see why his ministry, Solutions for Integrating Church and Home Education, has been well received in a number of churches that were skeptical about or having difficulties with home education.

The twofold goal of Solutions is to enable churches to: (1) do a better job in training all parents to become spiritual leaders for their children; and (2) offer effective programs to minister to those within their congregation who choose to home educate.

Solutions, through Eric and others, has now ministered to over 350 churches to help them in one or both of these major areas. Solutions has begun hosting seminars for church leaders to help equip pastors and others to be able to understand and make progress in developing a more effective whole family and home school ministry.

Eric did not begin by teaching other churches. Rather, Eric started in 1989 as the director for Harvester Teaching Services for Harvester Presbyterian Church in Springfield—a position he still holds. Harvester Teaching Services is like several of the "support groups of the future" we described in Chapter 2. It has a resource room, field trips, and a variety of other services and activities. But there is one unique feature: Harvester serves about 125 families—but only 100 of them home school. Eric's goal includes a desire to help single moms with the academic as well as spiritual concerns their children have—even though the circumstances of life make it difficult or unlikely they will ever home school. Many two-parent, non–home schooling families receive supplemental academic services as well. But the core of the ministry to non–home schooling families is spiritual help and encouragement to undertake the spiritual training of their child in a systematic way.

My own church, Blue Ridge Bible Church, VA, is definitely a home school–friendly church. Most, but not all, families with school-age children are home educators. I can tell you first-hand that a church like this has some definite advantages as well as definite disadvantages.

We have a strong desire to reach out to unchurched people in our community. But we don't want them to have to swallow home schooling as a price of getting in the door. Home schooling is not preached directly, and is referred to only in passing in our church services. We have Sunday School Classes and even a Youth Group—composed of almost all home school teens. For the vast majority of the time, the Youth Group has been led either by a home schooling couple or some home school alumni who are a year or two out of high school (operating under adult supervision).

From my own church's experience, as well as my exposure to the collective experience of various churches, let me suggest five principles that will help to define a home school-friendly church.

A "Compassionate" Church

1. Ways to become a home school–friendly church. Parent educators readily agree that "there is no one correct method for home schooling children." If we recognize the need for a variety of academic approaches, it shouldn't be too hard to accept that there are many ways to operate a church so that we can feel comfortable in it.

Some of us seem so absolutely certain that our particular practice is the perfect way of doing things that we become, in all candor, insufferable. I think just a bit more humility is appropriate. If God had wanted everyone to do things exactly our way, He would have easily directed one of the writers of the sixty-six books in the Bible to put the instructions down in precise language. Twenty years ago almost none of the Christians in America read Scripture to reach the conclusions we now have reached. Even in those areas where I think I am positively right, it is a matter of pride for me to suggest that other people's practices are unbiblical. I believe God has been gracious enough to allow us to live in an age in which we have been blessed to be part of a movement that expands our spiritual understanding in a positive way. Our proper response to God's graciousness to us should be to make us abundantly gracious to others.

A "Flexible" Church

2. *Hostilities to home schoolers should cease.* I can think of no good reason why a church wouldn't want to show enough flexibility to make it easy for home schoolers to be part of their church. I quite understand why a pastor would be reluctant to have abrasive "my way or the highway" home schoolers in his church. But the problem is their obnoxiousness, not the fact that they are home schoolers.

It is hostile and unacceptable to coerce people to put their children into Junior Church if they want them to be with them during the church service. But what if they make a fuss? To some degree my answer is to remember what Jesus said when the disciples tried to keep a bunch of presumptively noisy children away from Him: "Let the children come unto Me and forbid them not." I think we need to lighten up a little. An occasional cry or whimper ought to be tolerated.

One thing that should be especially tolerated, and even encouraged, is for children to be allowed to color or draw during church services. It is too much to ask children to sit still for over an hour. And it is not as if coloring distracts them from paying attention! I attend a lot of meetings, many of which I chair. When I do chair a meeting, I pay attention, careful attention, to what is being said. But I often come back from a meeting with my notepad full of scribbles and doodles. Was I not paying attention when I was doodling? On the contrary, doodling helped me to concentrate.

However, children who are disruptive ought to be removed by their parents from the church service. If the parent wants to stay with the child, so be it.

No home schooling teen should be made to feel like a second-class citizen if either the teen or the parents choose not to participate in a church's youth group activities. There is no duty to support church ministries, even for church staff, if the youth group practices violate the family's standards. Church leaders should be gracious and tolerant of those with stricter standards than those of the church.

This same spirit of toleration ought to be the standard even for churches with a Christian school.

An "Accommodating" Church

3. A church should minister to home schooling families.
For a church to attract home schoolers in the future, it is going to require a better marketing strategy than mere toleration and noncoercion. Church leaders should seriously consider some of the examples in this chapter—especially that of Westwood Baptist Church. What is wrong with having an age-integrated class as one of the Sunday School selections?

If a church adopts this kind of flexibility in its programs, especially if it either operates a home school support group or allows an independent group to use church facilities, somewhere between one-half and two-thirds of home schoolers will be quite happy.

Churches have gone to great lengths to create elaborate church growth plans. Becoming a home schooling accommodating church represents a strategy that has little cost and little downside risk and a tremendous opportunity for church growth.

A "Family-Centered" Church

4. A church should equip parents to teach spiritual truth to their children, rather than learning from church leaders in family-segregated settings. This is a high-risk strategy for many churches. All of us love doing the same old things so much we rarely ask ourselves if something completely different might not work better. And we almost never ask ourselves the even harder question, "Can we really justify our current practices in light of Scripture?"

A church like Bob Roach's, which is intensively family centered without wearing home schooling like a chip on its shoulder, has the greatest chance for real growth. All parents are looking for ways to become better spiritual educators of their children, and some of them will choose home schooling.

John Thompson's church is going to become a model as well. I believe that normally such churches will be small. Many home schoolers themselves would prefer another variety even if a family-intensive, home school–intensive church like Grace Bible Fellowship was available. There is nothing wrong with a modest- or moderate-sized church that fully meets the needs and desires of a goodly percentage of home schooling families. Such churches will proliferate, grow, and produce a number of outstanding children.

A "Family-Friendly" Youth Group

5. Youth groups, dating, and "over the edge" activities. We have talked about Sunday School classes being an issue. While some home schoolers have a problem with the whole concept of age segregation, the vast majority of home schoolers would not mind their children meeting once a week with other children in a Bible class *so long as the other children were required to meet reasonable standards of behavior.*

Finding a similar solution to youth groups is much more problematic. Our church's youth group offers an alternative. The vast majority of kids in the group are home schooled, dating is not practiced by any of the participants, and the leaders are committed to supporting a family-centered philosophy.

But perhaps the most realistic answer for most home schooling families would be to have a youth group that operates independently of their church. After all, groups like Young Life have done exactly this for decades. A form of Young Life that eschews a dating environment is one realistic possibility for spiritual training for teens.

It is possible for churches to adopt some sort of middle ground. The ground rules would have to include slightly higher standards than many youth groups follow. But most importantly, the youth group would have to forego any dating-oriented outings—Valentine's couples banquets and the like.

This is an area where church leaders need seriously to ask themselves: Can we justify the way we operate our youth group in the light of Scripture? When we encourage our kids to play flirtation games, how does that square with Jesus' teaching that a person who lusts in his or her heart has already committed adultery?

Many churches that reach happy accommodation with home

schooling families may find that suddenly the relationship flares into controversy when the oldest child in the family turns thirteen. Both sides will be far better off if a decision is made at the earliest possible moment as to which philosophy is going to prevail.

6

Equal Access to Public School Activities

I n the fall of 1996 Jason Taylor's parents installed an extra phone line in their home. They were getting so many calls from professional sports agents wanting to represent their son in the upcoming NFL draft that they needed the extra line.

Jason Taylor was a defensive star for the football team at the University of Akron for all four years of his college experience. And Jason was a high school standout in both basketball and football while growing up in the suburbs of Pittsburgh, Pennsylvania.

There are many student–athletes who make the transition from high school to college and then into professional athletics. But Jason Taylor is the first home schooler in America to do so. And, yes, Jason Taylor was home schooled through high school.

His college athletic experience almost never happened—not because of any lack of physical skills, but because the NCAA ruled Jason to be academically ineligible during his first week of football practice at Akron in the fall of 1992.

This ruling came as a total shock to Jason's parents and coaches because Jason's GPA throughout high school averaged 3.7 on a 4-point scale, and his SAT score was 70 points *higher* than the minimum required by the NCAA. Jason's sole deficiency came from the fact that he had been home schooled.

I got a call from Jason's parents asking if there was anything we could do to help convince the NCAA to reverse itself. The assistant athletic director at Akron, Rob Fournier, spoke to me on the phone and encouraged me to pursue the matter, promising the university's full support.

After about a week of intense negotiation while we prepared a lawsuit to file in federal district court, the NCAA reversed itself—largely because the Taylors had enrolled Jason in Christian Liberty Academy throughout his high school career and it had been third parties, rather than his parents, who had awarded Jason his 3.7 GPA.

Within ten years, virtually every school district in America will allow home schooled students to participate in sports and other extracurricular activities.

The legal issues that were present in the potential litigation against the NCAA were interesting, however, and I believed we would probably have prevailed had it been necessary to go to court. But I was both a little amazed and grateful at the outcome.

My amazement was even greater that Jason had been allowed to play football and basketball for Woodland Hills High School. In the vast majority of America's 16,000 school districts, Jason Taylor would have been allowed to watch only from the general admission bleachers. This is going to change. Within ten years, virtually every school district in America will allow home schooled students to participate in sports and other extracurricular activities. And in the majority of districts, home schooled students will also be allowed to enroll part-time to take one or more classes—chemistry, band, calculus, or driver's education.

For home schooled students to acquire public school sports eligibility, state legislatures will have to act to override the policies of state athletic associations. Local school districts normally do not have a realistic choice in the matter. If they allow home schooled students to

play on their teams, the state athletic associations will deem them ineligible for participation.

A number of cases have been brought in court over the years on
behalf of private school students who have wanted to play on public
school sports teams. These lawsuits have been uniformly unsuccessful,
and there is little reason to believe that home schools would fare much
better. (Massachusetts has provided an exception to this rule, but at a
high price, which will be discussed below.)

Political action in state legislatures is the only realistic way to
change the policy of state athletic associations. The normal opposition
from the public school establishment can be overcome if the home
schooling movement is united. But that is a growing difficulty because
a fissure has developed between "pro-sports bill" and "anti-sports bill"
contingencies within the home schooling community.

While a few home schooling pioneers are in the "pro-sports bill"
camp, the bulk of those embracing this trend for the future of home
education will be the new families that will fill the ranks of our movement. The majority of the seasoned veterans of the home schooling
movement are against "sports bills." Those home schoolers who wish
to have their state or school district adopt a policy allowing for equal
access for their children need to understand and deal with the arguments of those who contend that such policies are dangerous.

I will attempt to describe accurately the arguments of those who
oppose equal access policies, since many of my closest friends hold
these views. Indeed a majority of the lawyers at HSLDA share the view
of the "loyal opposition." But I am not among them. I'll explain my
reasons for favoring such bills as well.

Home School Participation in Public School Sports

Argument 1. Sports bills can be used to curtail the freedom of all home schoolers.

It is natural for public high schools to want to ensure that those who
are choosing to play on their teams meet the standards for academic

eligibility. Otherwise, a student who is failing in the traditional school could avoid academic disqualification simply by declaring himself to be a new "home schooler," and his parents could claim that he was doing fine.

To prevent such a misuse of home school participation in sports there has to be some kind of mechanism to ensure that the home schooling student is making true progress in his or her academic studies.

In the process of writing the necessary legislation to set the academic standards for sports participation it might occur to the education establishment that this might be an opportune time to seek to impose greater restrictions on all home schoolers—even on those who have no interest in participating in public school sports programs.

Many states do not impose the same level of scrutiny on home schooling programs in general that is likely to be imposed on home schoolers who want to play on the high school football team.

Home schoolers who want to play for public schools may bring about greater regulation of all families. And that is a great danger.

The danger is especially strong in states where home schools are treated as small private schools for legal purposes. In those states the private school laws are generally quite lenient. Any "home school sports" legislation would have to start with a definition of home schooling—and this would lead to a change in the general law on home schooling, which could result in severely curtailing everyone's freedom.

My comments. I agree with portions of this argument. No legislation which is written to allow public school sports participation should contain any provision imposing the same degree of public school scrutiny on all home schoolers. If the legislation does contain such a general regulation, then all home schoolers should join together for the bill's defeat. And I agree that there is special danger to those who live in "private school only" states.

However, in the eight states that have acted to allow home schoolers to play in public school sports teams, none of these policies mention home school. There is no reason to believe that "sports participation" laws could not be written with the same degree of protection in the other forty-two states.

In "private school only" states, the law could not be written so as to allow only home school students to participate without endangering their underlying legal right to operate as a small private school. In such states, legislation or policies would have to be written to allow sports participation for all private school students—or for all private schools of a certain size. For example, allowing eligibility for private school students from schools with fewer than ten students in grades 9 through 12 would allow all home schoolers to play—and few others. (I would not be opposed to allowing greater latitude for other small private schools, but that is a matter the private school advocates would need to work through.)

Argument 2. Those who want to play sports can find alternatives to public school participation.

Many home school support groups have fielded some very successful sports team programs. The Houston area home school basketball team is one of the top high school teams in Texas and competes regularly against the best public and private high schools. Virginia Beach and San Antonio both have excellent and quite comprehensive sports programs for home school students only.

Many traditional private schools also allow home schoolers to play on their teams as well as participate in a great variety of activities. Certainly, Christian home schoolers have more in common with their brothers and sisters in Christian private schools than they do with secular public schools. Students on sports teams face all manner of temptation from the new associations and friendships they make with their fellow players. Certainly they would be better off developing relationships with those on Christian school teams.

My comments. Again, I agree with many of the points. But it is simply untenable to suggest that most home schoolers have the kinds of opportunities that are available in Houston, Virginia Beach, and San Antonio.

It is also difficult to suggest that the private school option works well for all families. My third daughter, Katie, plays high school sports for Leesburg Christian High School (LCHS). We had thought of trying to get the law changed in Virginia so she could play for our local public high school. But that proved to be a political impossibility within the time frame, so we searched for alternatives and found a very good experience at LCHS. At this point if we were able to choose between the public school and the Christian school, we would choose the Christian school for the very reasons raised by the opponents of public school "sports bills" in the preceding section.

The opportunity to play for a Christian school team is not universally available. Some students don't live near such a school. In fact, we had great difficulties with the driving duties for Katie. It would have been a whole lot easier to drive Katie two miles to the public school than twelve miles each way to the Christian school. Now that she is sixteen, that is essentially solved, but any parent who faces transportation difficulties has my greatest sympathy.

Others live near enough to Christian schools, but the schools will not allow students to play on their teams. Sometimes the position is chosen by the leadership of the local school; other times the decision is made by the sports league in which the school participates.

Additionally, many sports are unavailable in even the biggest and best of private or home schools. For example, no home school program (at least to my knowledge) has a high school football team.

If we are truly going to make all sports available to all home school students, there is currently no realistic alternative to a public school sports participation bill.

Argument 3. Christian students should have nothing to do with secular schools.[1]

In the many discussions I have had with home school friends who oppose sports legislation, this is the argument on which they most rely.

Christians, they argue, should have nothing to do with secular

---

[1] I would like to remind my political critics who routinely quote my material against me, that in Argument 3 I am, once again, giving the arguments of those who assert a position with which I disagree.

government-run schools. After all, neither the Bible nor the Constitution gives any role to the government in providing a system of education. The secular schools indoctrinate children in the values of secular humanism, and by using and participating in these schools, we join with forces that not only keep God and prayer out, but also affirmatively teach evolution and numerous other anti-Christian principles throughout the school year.

By allowing our children to play on the teams from such schools, we are affirming and approving these teachings and approaches to education. Home schoolers should defeat sports legislation. Supporting such legislation acknowledges the legitimacy of the government schools that have become callous in their morality and antagonistic in their approach to God.

My comments. I have chosen to give my children a Christian education through home schooling because I believe that I have a responsibility to provide a Bible-centered education. Thus I could not in good conscience send my children to a system that fails to provide an affirmatively Christian education.

It is one thing for a parent to reject the substantive approach of secular education—which, by definition, leaves God out. It is another to allow our children to play on a secular sports team.

I have no quarrel with those who conclude that it would be improper for them to have their children play on a secular sports team. I would just point out that Little League is also secular and most Little League games are played on government fields operated by parks departments.

My biggest disappointment is that those who object to sports legislation seem so willing to impose their parental philosophy on everyone else's children. If they don't want their own children to play—fine. But their opposition to such legislation grows out of a view that they have reached a better decision for my children than I would have reached on my own.

One of the key principles of home schooling freedom is that parents have the sole legitimate authority to make decisions for their own children. We reject the government's power to make academic choices for our children. We reject the liberal nannyism of the Children's Defense Fund that wants to impose its UN-approved parenting philosophy on all of us. Why then would some home schoolers suddenly decide that they should be the nannies for other home schoolers who make different choices? Either we believe in parental freedom of decision or we don't.

If our desire is to promote home schooling for the widest group possible, we need to recognize that many families want their children to have these kinds of sports opportunities. Hundreds of students are enrolled in public schools each year because the family has made a decision that was prompted by a desire to play sports. Most of these people would have continued to home school if they would have had an option to pursue

> **Political action in state legislatures is the only realistic way to change the policy of state athletic associations.**

sports. And tens of thousands of husbands resist their wives' desire to home school their children because they want their son to play football or baseball. Maybe these people aren't as committed as most of the pioneers of the home schooling movement—but so what? Home schoolers shouldn't insist on ideological purity as a condition of entry. Our movement needs to meet people where they are and try to organize our legal and political options so that all families who are willing to work hard will have the realistic option of home schooling their children.

The Current State of Sports Law

One parent, Gary Lineburg, cornered me at a home schooling conference in Oregon in 1988 because he wanted HSLDA to bring a lawsuit so that his son could play high school sports. I told him that I didn't think it was possible to win such a lawsuit at that time. His only chance, I told him, was to approach the state legislature and get it to pass a bill allowing sports participation by home schooling students.

He did just that, and Oregon was one of the first states in the country to enact legislation allowing students to play on sports teams statewide. His cause was materially aided by the fact that Oregon's sister state, Washington, had an even broader law in place. When Washington State passed its original home schooling law in 1985, a provision was included allowing home schooling students to participate part-time in any public school course or extracurricular activity. Home schoolers in Washington State can enroll in algebra, band, gymnastics—or any course they desire.

One Arizona home schooling mom approached her state legislator and simply asked, "Why can't my son play sports on the local public school team?" Without any lobbying campaign, this legislator took the idea and saw it through until it was signed into law by Governor Fife Symington.

Colorado, Idaho, and Florida have also passed home school "sports bills". Iowa has a "dual enrollment" law that works much like the Washington program—students can enroll in any class or activity at the public school. Maine has a law which overrides the state athletic association ban on home schoolers, but leaves the issue of implementing the policy up to each local school district. The school is allowed, but not required, to include home schoolers on their public school teams.

The Future of Public Access

In the early fall of 1996 the *Washington Post* carried a featured story on the Falls Church (Virginia) School District which had reversed a previous policy allowing home schoolers to participate in band and other extracurricular activities. The reaction from the general public was overwhelmingly opposed to the school district's action. By late November of the same year, the school board again opened up many of its programs to home schooling students over the strenuous object of the district superintendent. Falls Church is in the midst of a liberal enclave in the most politically liberal part of the Washington, D.C., suburbs. The police cars in Falls Church are Volvos—no joke. If home school students can win the opportunity to participate in public school activities in Falls Church, they can win anywhere.

This trend will catch fire nationally in just a few years. Public school officials who care about students will support it. Those whose first love is the public school system will oppose it. But the justice of allowing students to participate is so self-evident that it will carry beyond Falls Church to the rest of the nation.

Those home schoolers who are afraid of the results of such legislation need to take the lead in drafting the bills. A new generation of home schoolers who want these kinds of services are rising. They will not accept the opinions some of our current leaders hold. New organizations will spring up to accommodate home schoolers who want this kind of participation if the old organizations insist on serving only those home schoolers who share their identical philosophy. It is far better for the existing organizations to adapt to the plurality of opinions on this subject and let those who want to participate do so while zealously protecting the rights of those who choose to avoid any contact with the public schools.

7

Apprenticeship Becomes a Real Choice

P arents who have thrown off the shackles of conventional thinking in providing their children with an education through high school are often willing to rethink the educational options for the college years as well. Talk of apprenticeship is a great fad in the home schooling community. Home schoolers warm to the idea that their children will be mentored by a competent professional who can provide on-the-job training with supplemental academic instruction in a course of training. Parents want their children to end up with both the recognized qualifications and the actual competence to assume the same career as the child's mentor.

The Virginia Department of Labor publishes a pamphlet on apprenticeship which sets forth the essence of this vision:

What is apprenticeship?

Apprenticeship has two parts:
On-the-job training (OJT) in the workplace.
OJT ensures that you will be fully trained in all areas of the occupation by a skilled professional.

Related instruction (RI) in the classroom after work.
RI builds the theoretical and technical knowledge you need for the
occupation. Usually, you will spend between four to six hours per week
in class.

Apprentices receive:

Certification. You will be awarded a certificate from the Common-
wealth of Virginia after successful completion of both the required
related instruction course and the on-the-job training.

Journeyman status. Successful completion of Apprenticeship
Training allows you to become a journeyman in your trade or craft.

As we will discuss more fully in just a bit, apprenticeship is alive and
well in this country for a number of occupations that would generally
be classified as "the trades." In fact, the Virginia law which sets up the
state's Apprenticeship Council includes the following restriction in the
definition of an "apprenticeable occupation": "It involves manual,
mechanical or technical skills which require a minimum of two thousand hours of on-the-job work experience of new apprenticeable
trades not otherwise established."

Traditional "blue collar" jobs are the primary focus of modern
apprenticeship programs. While these jobs provide a good and honest
living for those who pursue them, there is no reason why the methodology of apprenticeship needs to be limited to careers of a manual or
mechanical nature.

My own training as a lawyer had many of the components of
apprenticeship theory. I attended Gonzaga School of Law in Spokane,
Washington, from 1973 through 1976. I had intended to go to school
elsewhere (I was on the waiting list of an Ivy League school and was
belatedly accepted at another top school in the West) and ended up
applying late at Gonzaga. I was accepted, but was granted admission
only to the night program since all the slots for the day program had
been filled. In retrospect, I am glad I applied late.

During my second and third years of law school, I worked

approximately thirty hours a week in a small law firm, initially doing legal research and a variety of small chores—jobs which huge law firms give to recent graduates and associates with a couple years' experience. For example, my first day on the job, I was handed a medical malpractice file, told to draft the basic legal pleadings and begin doing the legal and medical research to back up the case.

Within a few weeks, I was doing a variety of tasks, some exciting (interviewing witnesses and writing briefs), some more mundane (serving subpoenas and making copies). And when the cases I was working on went to court, I was there with my boss helping out in a variety of ways, grateful for the experience and itching for the day I could stand up and argue in court on my own.

That day came sooner than might be expected. Under Washington State law, third-year law students can become "legal interns" and are allowed to participate in a variety of courtroom activities. In municipal courts (and other similar courts of limited jurisdiction) I was allowed as a legal intern to try traffic tickets, misdemeanors, and civil lawsuits up to a certain monetary threshold. In the state

> **The apprenticeship track is not only for blue-collar jobs, but also for most of the professional careers as well.**

superior court, which is the higher level trial court, I was permitted to argue motions and cases in open court in the presence of my supervising attorney. I was also allowed to present uncontested matters in either court by myself. I appeared in court in dozens of cases, most of them by myself, before I ever graduated from law school.

There is no question but that the value of my law school instruction was greatly enhanced by my simultaneous on-the-job training. The classes were not mere theory. I had a need to know because I was already in the field and could see the real life relevance of the instruction.

Most law students have only a limited opportunity to gain any kind of courtroom experience. Traditionally, the opportunity is limited to participation in moot court, which is a form of debate in the law school setting. Moot court is an exercise in which the student presents a brief and oral argument before a mock Supreme Court of the United States.

I participated in moot court in both my second and third years of law school. The week before the finals in my third year, I was in court Monday through Friday working, under the supervision of my boss, as the prime "attorney" in a business fraud case. On Saturday, I was in the moot court finals—and one of the seven judges on our panel was the same judge who had been listening to me all week in his real court-room. One could say that I was using a real trial to warm up for the pre-tend case. (I won the moot court championship and lost the fraud case.)

As a legal intern I appeared in court to argue for possession of a dead body on the theory that the dead man's wife was an accessory to his murder. I had sleuthed out the facts, subpoenaed the witnesses, written the brief, and argued the case against one of Spokane's best trial lawyers. My motion was granted.

I was sworn in as a lawyer on a Friday afternoon. The following Monday I started, by myself and against two opposing lawyers, a week-long real estate fraud trial before a jury. The jury awarded my client nearly every dollar I asked for. No law firm in the country would let a lawyer try a case like that solo on his first day of practice—unless he had had the kind of intensive training that my legal internship (apprenticeship if you will) had provided.

I have seen first-hand the value of a program that combines class-room instruction with on-the-job training that leads to a real and mar-ketable skill.

My daughter Jayme has also been "apprenticed." After graduating from high school at fifteen, she began to work as a graphic arts trainee under the tutelage of HSLDA's experienced senior graphic artist Darby Waters. For two years, Darby taught Jayme on the job, making the most of Jayme's natural talent with good instruction and practical experience. Then Darby left HSLDA to become a wife and mother. After a little looking, it was obvious that Jayme was more qualified to do the actual work than any of the college graduates in graphic arts that we interviewed.

Apprenticeship works. And the evidence is not limited to two members of the Farris family. Take the entire nation of Switzerland as an example.

Switzerland is a small nation, and its business leaders will tell you that the secret of their economic success lies, not in an abundance of natural resources, but in their people. Switzerland has managed to achieve the highest per capita income in the world without huge reserves of oil, coal, or iron—or even enough land to become an agricultural power. Business leaders say that two factors make their people productive: a workforce that is (1) highly educated and (2) committed to a strong work ethic.

In the United States 86 percent of students graduate from high school and approximately 60 percent of this group go on to some form of college instruction. In Switzerland only 25 percent graduate from high school, but almost all go on to college.

The balance—approximately 75 percent of the Swiss population—go into apprenticeship around age fifteen at the end of the rough equivalent of our eighth or ninth grade. Their apprenticeship programs, run by various private employers, consist of approximately half on-the-job training and half time in some type of formal instruction. The apprenticeship track is not only for blue-collar jobs, but also for most of the professional careers as well.

Swiss bankers, engineers, accountants, and scientists have risen to the top levels in their professions having come, not from college, but from corporate apprenticeship programs. Two of the three presidents of the largest Swiss banks entered their professions as apprentices.

This is a remarkable achievement for people with eight or nine years of classroom instruction. It says something quite dramatic about the failure of American public education. Few of our high school graduates would be academically prepared to begin the Swiss apprenticeship programs. In fact, many American college graduates would be on a par—not with the graduates of the apprenticeship programs—but with the students who are ready to enter.

Swiss public education has a far greater rate of success than does its American counterpart in its ability to prepare students for the work world. There are two reasons for this. One is that there is virtually no national educational bureaucracy. Schools are run at the local and cantonal level. And the second reason, in my opinion, is even more important: Swiss teachers are regularly on the ballot. These teacher elections are not "Renata v. Karin," but the question put to the parents and neighbors of each local school is: Do we retain Renata's contract?

Teachers are rarely voted out of office. Why? Because they understand the power of parents and neighbors. One disgruntled parent with an axe to grind can be nullified by his or her neighbors who have had good experiences with the teacher. But if a teacher consistently does a poor job, the parents have the power to rise up and send the teacher on his way.

In short, Swiss public education has been much more successful than American education because of its low bureaucracy and because the principle of parent-controlled education has real substance. I have been in Switzerland over twenty times in the past few years and have numerous Swiss friends. I believe our home school graduates compare favorably with their public school graduates, but whereas American home schoolers routinely outdistance their American public school counterparts, they do not outdistance the Swiss in any academic sense.

> **Home schooling is rapidly growing to the point where we will have 100,000 students a year who are ready to enter apprenticeship opportunities—and most would do so as an alternative to college.**

Those who make their living operating colleges will interject that not only do colleges prepare students for a career, they also prepare them for life by offering a liberal arts education. Most home schoolers are leery of most colleges for that very reason. Home schoolers' concerns do not arise from the mere offering of a liberal arts education. After all, I have gone to considerable length in Chapter 1, Classical Education Comes Home, to demonstrate that a philosophically sound liberal arts education taught in a traditional manner should be the essence of secondary education at home. It is not that home schoolers don't want their children taught philosophy, it is that they don't want their children taught the politically correct philosophy that dominates virtually all secular colleges and a great number of professing Christian colleges.

And it's not just home schoolers. Most parents want their children to go to college to prepare for a career. Let's read the great books in high school. And then let's prepare ourselves for the work world in college. That would emerge as the dominant inner conviction of most American parents of all stripes if they were given fifteen minutes of instruction on the options and a realistic choice in the matter.

Low bureaucracy/high parental involvement is the form of education that produces students who are ready to go into a workforce program of apprenticeship. Home schooling is rapidly growing to the point where we will have 100,000 students a year who are ready to enter apprenticeship opportunities—and most would do so as an alternative to college. There is only one significant barrier. The opportunities for true apprenticeship programs, outside of the trades–skill area, are so rare as to be essentially nonexistent.

Home schoolers should not ignore the existing trades-oriented apprenticeship opportunities. There are some 367,000 apprentices employed in programs registered with the U.S. Department of Labor. The vast majority of these apprentices are in career fields such as carpentry, masonry, electricity, machinery, mechanics, plumbing, and the like. (One should note that there are large numbers in cosmetology and barbering as well.) But since the early 1980s, there is a definite trend toward a high-tech orientation in apprenticeship, according to Rubin Dominguez, the deputy director of the Department of Labor's Bureau of Apprenticeship and Training.

Many traditional trades, such as machinists and draftsmen, are becoming high-tech in these apprenticeship programs. Computer-assisted drafting is the future of on-the-job draftsmen; so naturally the better apprentice programs use this methodology in training their new members.

A number of new high-tech fields are becoming available for apprentices as well. Virginia, for example, has 484 apprentices in registered programs to become computer-peripheral equipment operators. Scanning the list of over three hundred occupations which are registered in Virginia's state-registered apprenticeship program reveals some interesting options that go beyond the traditional construction or mechanical trades.

> Airplane inspector
> Audio-video repairer
> Computer-peripheral equipment operator
> Dental assistant
> Firefighter
> Furniture designer
> Jeweler
> Legal secretary
> Nurse (licensed practical)
> Dispensing optician
> Photographer (motion picture or still)
> Police officer
> Radio station operator

Rubin Domingez says that apprenticeship opportunities through government-registered programs are advertised in local public schools, unions, community organizations, and state or local government employment services. He was positive that local or state home schooling organizations could be added to the list of community groups that receive these broadcast announcements. Interested home schooling graduates could then compete for the eligible slots along with other applicants from the more traditional sources. Attached in the appendix is the address of all regional offices of the U.S. Department of Labor's apprenticeship program as well as the office for all states that have such offices. (Sorry, telephone numbers were not available to me.) Every state home schooling organization and most support groups should endeavor to get on the mailing list for these announcements so that our students will know about potential openings. The programs are government registered, but offered almost exclusively by private employers.

Domingez was quick to point out that registration of apprenticeship programs is voluntary in our country and many programs operate outside the government system. One of the reasons they make this choice, Domingez said, was the "perceived difficulties" with the paperwork and so on that is required because of the government's affirmative action programs.

I asked Domingez why America had not found a way to offer some of the professional careers through apprenticeship that are so popular in Switzerland, Germany, and other European nations. He indicated that in our country there are no tax breaks for employers who offer such programs.

If the current Republican Congress wanted to offer a legitimate school-to-work program (as opposed to the socialistic, government-dictated model that has been on the scene for the past few years), they should adopt some generous tax breaks to companies that offer apprenticeship opportunities. Other than that the government should get out of the way.

Many home schoolers want far more than the ability to participate in existing apprenticeship programs. We want to use this model of training available to enable our graduates to become doctors, lawyers, engineers, accountants, pastors, and journalists. With only trivial exceptions, these career choices are simply not available today through the apprenticeship model.

One program that has generated a lot of interest in home schooling circles is the Oak Brook School of Law which is operated as an affiliate to Bill Gothard's Advanced Training Institute. I serve on the advisory board (which is a list of endorsers rather than a governing board) for this school and am friends with most of the members of the faculty. The professors for this school are top-notch, and all have the ability and most have the credentials to teach at well-known law schools.

Oak Brook is a correspondence law school that requires its students to attend a short introductory course in person. The program takes four years and is registered with the California system, and it allows its graduates to take only the California bar.

Oak Brook is required by California law to impose a requirement of two years of college for entry into the school. The school strongly encourages those without the college education requirement to take and pass the necessary examinations to attain the college credits. I know several young men who have been accepted at Oak Brook who have never attended a day of college classes, but who simply took the various CLEP tests and were awarded two years' credit.

Like all correspondence law schools in California, Oak Brook students must take the "baby" bar examination after the first year of their instruction. The students are not allowed to go on to the second year until they have passed this examination.

The overall pass rate for the 1996 baby bar was 16.5 percent for all students taking the exam. Oak Brook saw 52.5 percent of its students pass—quite a commendable record!

However, after graduation Oak Brook graduates are allowed to take only the California bar examination. Once the graduates pass this examination, it is at least possible that some states will allow Oak Brook graduates to use their status as a California lawyer to take the bar examination for other states. That possibility should be checked out well in advance.

The only way to waive another state's bar is for the graduate to practice law in California for five years and then move to another state. And very few states will let California lawyers "waive in," even if they graduate from Harvard or Stanford.

My biggest concerns about the Oak Brook program are not about the bar opportunities, but about the nature of correspondence study for the study of law.

Standing alone, correspondence study provides an adequate way to get the academic knowledge necessary to become a good lawyer. But, in my judgment, it is not nearly as good as traditional law schools in this regard. (Oak Brook fans, keep reading before you react.)

But if an Oak Brook student is actively working for a lawyer or judge and doing legal research and assisting with clients, then the full component of the apprenticeship model is operating. Academic instruction from Oak Brook, plus real live on-the-job training and experience, is, in my opinion, superior to a traditional law school program which is so dominantly academic in its orientation.

Making Apprenticeship a Reality

1. Modern "masters" should lead the way.

In colonial days the masters who trained apprentices had a clear economic incentive for this training. At first the apprentice was often more trouble than he was worth. But as the training and experience proceeded, the apprentice became more and more useful to the master. At some point the apprentice became an economic asset rather than a time-consuming liability.

Business owners and managers need to open their minds and consider whether some of the positions traditionally reserved for college graduates might not be filled with an apprenticeship approach. Consider one example for my experience as president of the HSLDA.

Several years ago we hired an eighteen-year-old home school graduate named Aaron Fessler to serve as an assistant office manager with a specific assignment—to work with our outside computer consultants to keep our systems running properly. Aaron had some basic computer knowledge and a great deal of aptitude. After a couple of years we were able to take more and more of the work away from the outside consultants and give it to Aaron. Eventually Aaron was writing customized software for us and was an important person in the firm.

We started Aaron at a modest pay scale—around $7 or $8 an hour—and gave him increases as a reward for his ability and responsibility. By the time Aaron was around twenty-two, he was earning an annual salary in the high 30s. But then Aaron took a giant step forward—he became a business owner with an ingenious product that gives giant companies and agencies an inexpensive way to access the Internet. Aaron has left our organization and is well on his way to becoming wealthy.

The experience he gained here was a tremendous asset for Aaron, and it allowed him to launch himself far ahead of virtually all college graduates. But it was a tremendously successful experience for the HSLDA as well—even if the experience were analyzed only from an economic perspective. We were able to get high-level labor at a low price. To find people who had the same level of computer skill as our twenty-three-year-old, we had to go into the market and interview candidates in their late thirties and early forties. And the market prices for these candidates was far above the last salary we paid Aaron, even though everyone concerned (including Aaron) thought he was being compensated quite generously for a person of his age. Thus for two or three years we had saved a great deal of money by using our on-the-job trained "kid" in lieu of a much higher priced professional who had been trained in the traditional manner.

It has been my experience that the success of any of the fifty or so employees that I supervise has little to do with whether or not they have a college education. Six months of on-the-job training with a person who is naturally bright, self-disciplined, willing to work hard, and has a positive attitude is more than a match for four years of college.

Many business owners and managers will probably agree with me. The trouble has been in finding a consistent supply of people who fill the criteria of being bright, positive, self-disciplined, and hard working. Such workers are rare finds among the population at large. I do not wish to give the impression that every home schooling graduate completely fills these criteria. But I would say that at least one-third of them could fill virtually any job normally given to those with bachelor's degrees if the employer would give them about six months of on-the-job training. That's about the same amount of time it requires most college graduates to become reasonably assimilated into the process and systems of any new job.

For two or three years employers can expect to pay a home school apprentice less than the market would require for an equally productive college graduate. It is clearly a good economic deal for both parties.

2. Churches should train pastors using the apprenticeship model.

Seminaries can teach Greek and Hebrew, homiletics, and survey of doctrine, but seminaries have proven to be singularly unsuccessful in teaching men to become good pastors. Pastoring is a people-intensive occupation, whereas seminary is an academic-intensive occupation. There certainly should be a way to gain the needed academics in a process that is far more people-intensive.

There is no reason why pastors could not be trained exclusively through the apprenticeship model. Any large church would have more than enough staff who are skilled in the languages and the necessary academic subjects. Denominations could operate apprenticeship programs even among smaller churches (which could use the help of apprenticeship pastoral staff) by rotating the apprentices from church to church through a four- or five-year cycle. The first year could be with a pastor who is a Greek scholar, the next year with a homiletics teacher, and so on.

With the advent of high technology, seminary specialization courses can be learned by video, direct broadcast satellite, or on the internet just as easily as in the traditional classroom.

Throughout this time, the apprentices would be learning the academic subjects as a sideline to the real skill in church leadership—learning to interact successfully with people.

A great number of men feel called into the ministry when they are a little older. Normally they already have a wife and a child or two. This is probably the best stage in life to become a pastor because the man normally has the maturity required for this challenging task. But it is also the most difficult stage in life to undertake a traditional academic program.

Many men struggle with the severe economic hardships that attending seminary places on their families. Far too many families disintegrate from the sheer economic pressures that seminary places on them. When the time commitment of studies and work are added, few families go unscathed. Marriages unravel, and children become alienated.

God's way of training church leaders should certainly not lead to family difficulties and divorce.

The economic costs to churches and denominations to maintain seminaries is not to be overlooked either. Even though students pay tuition and fees, there is always a need for the denomination to underwrite the substantial costs of the institution. Millions of dollars are being spent for buildings and instructors that could be better invested in church work that both trains new pastors and brings needed services to people now. Rather than building that new seminary classroom, the denomination could rent that inner-city tutoring center and put the pastor–apprentice in charge.

Training pastors in the apprenticeship model yields several advantages: (1) academics are learned in the context of people-skill training; (2) churches get needed help for the cost of sustenance wages; (3) there is no disadvantage to being mature before entering the pastoral training; and (4) the pressures on marriages and families are greatly reduced. In short, training pastors in the apprenticeship model produces better pastors and a better experience for those who want to become pastors at a lower cost.

3. We should start numerous apprenticeship model programs.

For apprenticeship to take its rightful place as the prime method to train people for careers, some brave individuals will have to step forward and start model programs which demonstrate that this method is mutually successful for the learner and the employer.

To that end, the organization I head has undertaken to plan an "apprenticeship college." We intend to launch at least two career training programs immediately, and another two careers in the future.

First, we will start an apprenticeship program for journalism. It is our desire to have a program that offers a mix of on-the-job training and academic instruction. We intend to launch either a newspaper or a news service (the Associated Press is one example of a news service) and hire a number of seasoned journalists who share our vision and worldview to become mentors for the journalist-apprentices. We envision the program lasting about two years. It will be structured so that at the end of the program the apprentices will have the skills and experiences needed to land real jobs reporting the news.

Second, we intend to start a similar program for legislative assistants. Our work on Capitol Hill has taught us that much of the real work of Congress takes place in the hearts and minds of the young people who serve as legislative assistants. Most of these "LAs" are recent college graduates with no particular training in either the substance or process of legislation—even if they are political science graduates.

In a two-year program of work on legislative analysis involving both real-life experience and academic training, we believe that we can train some of the best congressional aides anywhere. We believe that those who complete our two-year apprenticeship program will have little difficulty in landing jobs as legislative assistants in either Congress or in state legislatures.

It should be obvious that we have chosen two careers that have a significant impact on our culture and that have been traditionally dominated by the Left. If we want to stop the liberal bias of most reporters, we need to train people who share our perspective on life to become excellent reporters. And if we want to stop the process in which a conservative legislator has to fight his own liberal staff to maintain his positions, we have to train some of the best and the brightest to become the best legislative aides available.

Our future plans involve the careers of law and business. But those will be a number of years down the road. Our programs of journalism and public policy will be up and operating well before the year 2000.

4. We need to publicize our successes.

Home schoolers publish hundreds of newsletters and magazines. We have radio shows. And we have many contacts in the media. Apprenticeship success stories are newsworthy. In these interesting, off-beat ways, people can succeed. A great number of people will be interested in hearing our stories.

One of the real purposes of telling these stories is to influence those who listen. A business owner who listens might be inspired to take on one or two apprentices to see how it works. A student who succeeds for himself, and for the business for which he or she works, will inspire others to investigate and act.

No apprenticeship story should go untold. If your child worked as a teller at age eighteen, and then to be promoted to a job traditionally given to college graduates, that story needs to be told.

For many people, apprenticeship is a hazy dream that seems a bit unreal. When we hear the stories of those who have broken the mold and have made it work, the haze will dissipate and we will all clearly see that this method of career preparation really works.

Postscript. If you want your children to be among those who can truly excel at the apprenticeship method of career preparation, the time to start training is early on. Inge Cannon has written some excellent materials that give many practical suggestions about how to build a home school education that will give the student both the experience and insight necessary to become a first-rate apprentice. Apprenticeship-Plus materials can be ordered at the following address:

Education PLUS
P.O. Box 1350
Taylors, SC 29687
(864) 609-5411

Ten Most Commonly Asked Questions About Home Schooling

1. What about socialization?

Anyone who has been home schooling longer than two weeks has been asked this question dozens of times. It was the first question I asked when I first heard of home schooling in 1982.

First of all, it is fair to say that home schooling does not eliminate socialization, but it does separate socialization and academics to a considerable degree. If one gives even five seconds of thought to that, it should be immediately recognized that this is a plus and not a minus for home schooling.

Do you want your child to be doing his algebra assignment while talking to his girlfriend on the telephone? Probably not. Common sense tells you that some separation of academics and socialization is a good idea.

Much of what goes on in public schools is an inappropriate mix of socialization and academics. Children whisper, slip notes to each other, gaze longingly at their latest flame, or do any number of socially oriented activities while the teacher is trying his or her best to impart some material. And it goes without saying that much of the socialization that is common these days is plainly wrong in any setting.

Drugs, alcohol, and premarital sex are all part of the socialization scene that home schoolers miss out on during their academic day (and to a great extent they miss out on these things altogether).

A good part of socialization is done at the right time and with the right people. Home schoolers are active young people in community sports, scouting, church activities, 4-H, political volunteering, community service, and more. When it is time to do academics, home schooled students do it with vigor. The same vigor is present with social contacts and service.

On a more technical level, socialization is properly understood by professional sociologists as the method by which we teach the next generation the rules of society. Do we really want six-year-olds responsible for socializing each other? Isn't it better for our children to learn the rules of society and the values that make society work from responsible adults? But the fact is that children get their socialization values from whomever they spend a majority of their time. If they spend the majority of their time with other six-year-olds, they get their fundamental values from their peers. If they spend a majority of their time with their parents and family, then parents are the source of that child's fundamental values. If you doubt this, project ahead until age fourteen or so. How many fourteen-year-olds are more influenced by their peers than their parents? I rest my case.

I knew home schooling socialization worked really well when I saw my oldest daughter Christy—at the age of fourteen!—carrying on an animated conversation over lunch in Paris as she sat between a priest from Portugal and a barrister from London. She was obviously able to get along with others from other age groups and other cultures.

Isn't that the real test of socialization—the ability to get along with people who are outside your immediate peer group?

The kind of socialization that results from peer-dependent institutional schools is contrary to the way all the rest of life works. Where else in society do people go around in packs of age-segregated herds?

And just in case you wonder whether Christy can get along with people her own age, she was elected student body vice president of her college.

Over the years I have developed the ultimate test for those concerned about socialization. Take twenty-five six-year-olds and one adult to a birthday party at McDonald's. Use a private side party room. Start a stop watch. See how long it takes the good part of group socialization to turn into a negative experience. It will be less than the six-hour period that is the typical school day.

If you home school, your children will not be social misfits. After 3:30 in the afternoon, your family will be like all others. I have had fifteen years' experience with my own family—let me assure you that your kids will turn out fine, just fine.

2. Where do I get curriculum information?

There are four basic sources for curriculum information: (1) home school conventions; (2) home school magazines; (3) state and local home school groups; and (4) two excellent sets of books which give a great deal of information about curriculum.

A list of state home schooling organizations is printed in Appendix B. They are the best sources for finding out about the home schooling conventions that put on curriculum fairs in a two- or three-day event. These are not small events. The California convention takes virtually all of the display space at the Disneyland Hotel. The Indiana convention is in the Hoosier Dome. There are dozens and dozens of suppliers offering thousands of different materials for home schoolers.

Many local support groups will have a regular program to offer curriculum advice (see Chapter 3 for a description of the support groups of the future). You can find these local groups via the state organizations.

Home schooling magazines have a number of different articles on curriculum choices and, of course, carry beneficial advertisements from the suppliers themselves.

The Teaching Home is the granddaddy of home schooling magazines in both size and longevity. It is an excellent resource for curriculum and general home schooling information. To subscribe, contact: The Teaching Home, P.O. Box 469069, Escondido, California 92046-9069, 1-800-395-7760. For information, contact: The Teaching Home,

P.O. Box 20219, Portland, Oregon 97294-0219, (503) 253-9633, http://www.teleport.com/~tth.

Other quality home schooling publications include: Practical Home-schooling, c/o HomeLife, P.O. Box 1250, Fenton, Missouri, 63026-1850, 1-800-346-6322, http://www.home-school.com and Homeschooling Today, P.O. Box 5863, Hollywood, Florida, 33083 (954) 962-1930, 74672.2004@compuserve.com, HSTodayMag@aol.com.

Two excellent resources have been on the market for years from two talented home schooling mothers, and are continuously updated.

Cathy Duffy's *Christian Home Educator's Curriculum Manual* (Home Run Enterprises, 1995) contains a usable description of numerous choices popular among home schoolers. It can be special-ordered from most book stores or by calling Home Run Enterprises at 714-841-1220 or by writing 16172 Huxley Circle, Westminster, CA 92683.

Mary Pride, who is also a committed evangelical Christian, has produced the aptly named *Big Book of Home Learning* (Crossway, 1996), which is really a multi-volume set. The prolific Pride has produced a resources review which includes both Christian and secular publications and materials in a witty and objective writing style. It can also be found or special-ordered in book stores or may be obtained by calling HomeLife at 1-800-346-6322.

3. How can I find a local support group?

Call one of the state organizations listed in Appendix B and ask for a support group in your area.

4. What are the best states for home schooling freedoms?

My two personal favorites are Montana and about half the counties in Virginia (which correctly interpret and apply both the regular home schooling law and the religious exemption statute).

The other six attorneys at HSLDA also recommend Montana, Missouri, Texas, and Oklahoma as having very good home schooling laws.

5. What are the worst states for home schooling freedoms?

I would not voluntarily choose to live under the home schooling laws of either Pennsylvania or New York. While these laws were a great improvement over the laws they replaced, both states should lighten up considerably.

The laws as written are not good in Rhode Island or Massachusetts because they vest discretion in the local officials to approve or disapprove a home schooling program. This is ameliorated in a number of states by application and interpretation. Rhode Island, for example, has a number of decisions from the commissioner of education which have interpreted a vague law in a manner that makes Rhode Island a livable state in actual practice.

California is a noteworthy state from a legal perspective. Many school officials believe that a teacher's certification requirement for home schooling is the current law. The HSLDA believes they are wrong. But there is a possibility of trouble in California if this wrong opinion gains momentum. In practice, there are more home schoolers in California than in any other state and most school districts leave home schoolers alone.

6. What do home schoolers do for high school graduation and college admission?

In 1982 I asked the only experienced home schooler I knew, Roger Schurke, where he would get a high school diploma for his oldest daughter. His answer? A print shop—the same place public schools get theirs.

The HSLDA has gone to a print shop and has produced a very nice leather-bound diploma with gold seals, which we sell for close to cost ($15) to any home schooler. Nothing prohibits a family from printing its own.

But the real question most potential home schoolers want to know is not where they get the piece of paper, but will their child's graduation be recognized for college admission or other similar purposes? The answer is yes, with qualifications.

Home schoolers have learned how to get admitted to virtually any college or university in the nation. Some colleges have aggressively recruited home schoolers because of the colleges' good experiences with prior home schooled students.

But a bit more is exacted than they require of a traditional high school graduate. In addition to the standard achievement tests (SAT or ACT), home schoolers are expected to provide good written documentation of the kind of course work they have done in the high school years and an explanation of the grades that have been assigned to the student. If a student has very high SAT scores, a parent's statement that the student has been an "A" student will be received fairly readily. There is more skepticism if a home schooler claims top grades and has low test scores.

Many home schooled students take a course or two during their high school years at a local junior college. If a student does well in these courses, then a four-year college or university will probably accept at face value a parent's assessment that the student has done well in his home-based courses as well.

7. How can I home school if I can't teach physics or calculus?

Relax. Most people don't need to be able to teach physics or calculus to their six- or-seven-year-olds. In fact, very few people study these courses in high school or college. So don't sweat it.

If you want your child to take these courses at sixteen or seventeen, a junior college is available today and on-line instruction is just around the corner (see Chapter 3).

But, the real question is: Can I give my child what he or she needs in the challenging high school courses?

First, consider a class that you could teach if you simply had a bit of a refresher. That was the way I was with teaching Algebra I to my two oldest daughters. I nearly panicked when on the first day of the school year I opened the algebra book into the middle and saw quadratic equations. I had no memory of how to do them. But I was more than capable of teaching the first several lessons and, as I went through it with my daughters, I began to remember the subject. By the time we got to quadratic equations I had relearned what I needed to know in order to impart the material each morning.

There is another kind of class—one that the parent has never learned. For this kind of class, which is almost exclusively a high school phenomenon, most families have enrolled at a friendly private school for a single class, a junior college, or hired a tutor. Again, the high-tech alternatives are on their way and will make most other choices for specialized classes obsolete.

8. Does home schooling have to be done by a parent?

While some state laws require a parent to teach his own child to be considered a home schooler, most have some alternative for a nonparent to do some or all of the teaching.

However, the vast majority of home schooling is done by mothers, with some assistance from the father.

A few grandparents also home school their grandchildren. Some aunts have taken in their nieces and nephews. But, outside of the immediate family, home schooling another person's child is extraordinarily rare.

In the Reagan–Bush years I used to meet regularly with officials from the Department of Education. Many were convinced of the validity of home schooling, and I got many requests for recommendations of people who would home school their children.

I do not recommend home schooling someone else's child (outside of meeting urgent needs of family) until your children are finished. Once your own children are gone, if state law permits it, I think an experienced home schooling mom could take in three or four children and charge about $12,000 a year each for private tutoring. In my opinion, that is the value of the undertaking in fair market terms.

9. How can one mother teach two or more children at the same time?

Have you ever heard of the one-room school house? National literacy was virtually universal when this kind of educational practice was common.

One teacher can juggle multiple lessons with multiple grades each day, but it takes some organization and practice.

Our family represents a high-end challenge. We currently have five children of school age. Basically, it takes about fifteen minutes to go over one subject with one child. That fifteen minutes will produce between fifteen minutes and an hour's worth of work for the child to do on his or her own.

My wife takes a two- or three-lesson block (thirty to forty-five minutes) with each child in the morning and a similar block in the afternoon. After they have received their assignments they are expected to go to another part of the house and do it while the next child is receiving his or her instruction.

We've been at this for fifteen years, and it works quite well.

10. What do I do with my toddlers while I am teaching my older children?

We have alternately used one of three alternatives over the years. First, all toddlers have mandatory nap time in the afternoon. Naps may or may not involve sleeping. But they will be in their room, and they will have their door shut—period.

If a mother is teaching only a first or second grader, for example, a two-hour nap will provide all the quiet time necessary for a great academic program.

Second, we have our older kids watch our younger kids for short blocks of time. Starting around age nine, our older children have taken thirty- to forty-five–minute blocks once a day watching the toddlers in a nearby room while their mother teaches. One block a day does not distract from the overall school work of the older child—but it doesn't have to be done on a rigid schedule as in conventional schools.

Third, for short periods toddlers can be kept occupied with their own "reading" or art projects or other activities that distract them and give them some purposeful activity at the same time.

Appendix A:
Home Schooling Reference Guide

Chapter One:
Classical Education Comes Home

The Lost Tools of Learning
Dorothy Sayers
National Review
215 Lexington Avenue
New York, NY 10016
(212) 679-7330

***Escondido Tutorial
Services***
Fritz Hinrichs
2634 Bernardo Avenue
Escondido, CA 92029
(760) 746-0980

Classical Education
Fritz Hinrichs
2634 Bernardo Avenue
Escondido, CA 92029
(760) 746-0980

Great Books
Fritz Hinrichs
2634 Bernardo Avenue
Escondido, CA 92029
(760) 746-0980

Worldviews of the Western World
Cornerstone Curriculum Project
2006 Flat Creek Place
Richardson, TX 75080
(972) 235-5149

Calvert School
105 Tuscany Road
Baltimore, MD 21210
(410) 243-6030

Konos
P.O. Box 250
Anna, TX 75409
(972) 924-2712

Progeny Press
200 Spring Street
Eau Claire, WI 54703
(715) 833-5259

Greenleaf Press
Rob Shearer
3761 Highway 109 North Unit D
Lebanon, TN 37087
(615) 449-1617

Trivium Pursuit
Harvey & Laurie Bluedorn
139 Colorado Street
Wuscatine, IA 52761
(309) 537-3641

Cedarville College
P.O. Box 601
Cedarville, OH 45314
(513) 766-2211

Chapter Two:
Broadening Our Political Horizons

Home School Legal Defense Association
P.O. Box 3000
Purcellville, Virginia 20134
(540) 338-5600
FAX (540) 338-2733

Broadman & Holman Publishers
127 Ninth Avenue, North
Nashville, Tennessee 37234
(615) 251-2000

Madison Project
P.O. Box 479
Hamilton, Virginia 20159
(540) 338-7575
FAX (540) 338-1998

Chapter Three:
Support Groups of the Future

Circle Christian School
Werner, Jim and Linda
4644 Adanson Street
Orlando, FL 32804
(407) 740-8877

Hearts at Home L.E.A.H.
(Loving Education At Home)
Foster, Brenda
P.O. Box 23
Fairport, NY 14450
(716) 377-9309

South Carolina
Association of Independent
Home Schools (SCAIHS)
Tyler, Zan
P.O. Box 7104
Irmo, SC 29063
(803) 551-1003

Home School Patriots
Eastis, John and Annette
P.O. Box 292242
Cunthelan, CA 92329-2242
(619) 868-5846

Joyful Sound Home School
Choir
Spencer, Paula
P.O. Box 5695
Kingwood, TX 77325
(281) 399-1362

Families Accountable for
their Children's Education
and Training (FACET)
Zook, Chris and Robin
6437 Galway Drive
Colorado Springs, CO 80918
(719) 593-7389

Olive Tree Christian School
Woodson, Donna
11586 Arguello Drive
Mira Loma, CA 91752
(909) 685-6325

Homes Organized for
Meaningful Education
(HOME)
Likes, Bob
9725 Babbitt Avenue
Northridge, CA 91325
(818) 993-5947

Keystone Academy
P.O. Box 1888
Norwalk, CA 90651-1888
(562) 862-7134

Saxon's Advanced
Mathematics
1320 West Lindsey
Norman, OK 73069
(405) 329-7071

Home School Legal Defense
Association
P.O. Box 3000
Purcellville, VA 20134
(540) 338-5600

NATional cHallenged
Homeschoolers Associated
Network (NATHHAN)
Bushnell, Tom and Sherry
5383 Alpine Road, SE
Olalla, WA 98359
(253) 857-4257

How a Man Prepares His
Daughters for Life
Bethany House Publishers
11300 Hampshire Ave. South
Minneapolis, MN 55438
(612) 829-2500

Family Protection
Ministries
910 Sunrise Avenue Suite A-1
Roseville, CA 95661
(916) 786-3523

Chapter Four:
High-Tech Learning

Utah State University
Department of
Instructional Technology
Smellie, Don, Department Head
Logan, UT 84322-2830
(801) 797-1000

Home School Computing
(section of The Teaching
Home Magazine)
Constable, Farren
P.O. Box 116
Blue Rapids, KS 66411
(800) 464-7797
http://www.webpress.net/ipk/hsc

HOMER
UOL Publishing
12372 River Ridge Ave.
Burnsville, MN 55337-1665
(800) 529-1606

North Dakota Department of Public Instruction
600 East Ave.
Bismarck, ND 58505-0440
(701) 328-2260

Megatrends
by John Naisbitt
Warner Books Inc.
330 World Trade Center
New York, NY 10048
(212) 775-1442

Escondido Tutorial Services
Hinrichs, Fritz
2634 Bernardo Avenue
Escondido, CA 92029
(619) 746-0980

Practical Homeschooling
Pride, Mary
P.O. Box 1250
Fenton, MO 63026
(800) 346-6322

Somerville, Scott
P.O. Box 3000
Purcellville, VA 20134
(540) 338-5600

Big Book of Home Learning
Pride, Mary
P.O. Box 1250
Fenton, MO 63026
(800) 346-6322

Syracuse Language Systems' Triple Play Plus
5790 Widewaters Parkway
Syracuse, NY 13214-2845
(800) 797-5264

Your Way 2.0 / Language Connect University
5790 Widewaters Parkway
Syracuse, NY 13214-2845
(800) 797-5264

Folio Bound Views Version 3.1a CD Sourcebook of American History
Folio Corporation
Provo, Utah 84604
801-229-6300

Barton, David
P.O. Box 397
Aledo, TX 76008
(817) 441-6044

Burkett, Larry
601 Broad Street, SE
Gainesville, GA 30501
(770) 536-1689

Chapter Five:
Home School–Friendly Churches

Westwood Baptist Church
Forstrom, Lee - Senior Pastor
333 Kaiser Road N.W.
Olympia, WA 98502
(360) 866-6888

Grace Bible Fellowship
Thompson, John - Teaching
Elder
Valley Road 651B
Walpole, NH 03608
(603) 445-5474

Calvary Worship Center
Roach, Bob - Pastor
500 S.W. Bethany Drive
Port St. Lucie, FL 34986
(561) 340-3923

Solutions for Integrating Church and Home Education
Wallace, Eric
P.O. Box 630
Lorton, VA 22199
(703) 455-5163

Harvester Presbyterian Church
Harvester Teaching Services
Wallace, Eric - Director
7800 Rolling Road
Springfield, VA 22153
(703) 455-7800

Blue Ridge Bible Church
P.O. Box 217
Purcellville, VA
(540) 338-2299

Chapter Six:
Equal Access to Public School Activities

Christian Liberty Academy
502 W. Euclid Ave.
Arlington Heights, IL 60004
(847) 259-8736

"A Sour Note for Home-
Schooler", *The Washington Post*,
Friday, August 23, 1996.

Chapter Seven:
Apprenticeship Becomes a Real Choice

Virginia Department of Labor
13 South Thirteenth Street
Richmond, VA 23219
(804) 786-2377
FAX (804) 371-6524

Apprenticeship Division of The Virginia Dept. of Labor & Industry
13 South Thirteenth Street
Richmond, VA 23219-401
(804) 786-2381

U.S. Department of Labor
200 Constitution Avenue, N.W.
Washington, DC 20210
(202) 219-5000

U.S. Department of Labor
Bureau of Apprenticeship and Training
200 Constitution Avenue, NW
Room N-4649
Washington, DC 20210
(202) 219-5921

Regional Offices, Bureau of Apprenticeship and Training, U.S. Department of Labor

LOCATION	STATES SERVED
Regional Director Region I Room E370 JFK Federal Bldg. Boston, Massachusetts 02203	Connecticut New Hampshire Maine Rhode Island Massachusetts Vermont

Regional Director	New Jersey
Region II	Puerto Rico
Room 602 - Federal Building	New York
201 Varick Street	Virgin Islands
New York, New York 10014	

Regional Director	Delaware
Region III	Virginia
Room 13240 - Gateway Bldg.	Maryland
3535 Market Street	West Virginia
Philadelphia, Pennsylvania 19104	Pennsylvania

Regional Director	Alabama
Region IV	Mississippi
Room 6 T71	Florida
61 Eursyth St., S.W.	North Carolina
Atlanta, Georgia 30303	Georgia
	South Carolina
	Kentucky
	Tennessee

Regional Director	Illinois
Region V	Minnesota
Room 708	Indiana
230 South Dearborn St.	Ohio
Chicago, Illinois 60604	Michigan
	Wisconsin

Regional Director	Arkansas
Region VI	Oklahoma
Room 628 - Federal Building	Louisiana
525 Griffin Street	Texas
Dallas, Texas 75202	New Mexico

Regional Director	Iowa
Region VII	Missouri
1100 Main Street	Kansas
Kansas City, Missouri 64105-2112	Nebraska

Regional Director	Colorado
Region VIII	South Dakota
Room 465	Montana
U.S. Custom House	Utah
721 - 19th Street	North Dakota
Denver, Colorado 80202	Wyoming

Regional Director	Arizona
Region IX	Hawaii
Federal Building, Room 715	California
71 Stevenson Street	Nevada
San Francisco, California 94105	

Regional Director	Alaska
Region X	Oregon
1111 Third Avenue	Idaho
Room 925	Washington
Seattle, Washington 98101-3212	

State Apprenticeship Councils and Agencies

Arizona
Apprenticeship Services
USDL-BAT
Suite 302
3221 North 16th St.
Phoenix, AZ 85016
(602) 640-2964

California
Division of Apprenticeship
USDL-BAT
Suite 1090 - N
1301 Clay Street
Oakland, CA 94612-5217
(510) 637-2951

Connecticut
Office of Job Training and Skill
Development
USDL-BAT
Federal Building
135 High Street - Room 367
Hartford, CT 06103
(203) 240-4311

District of Columbia
D.C. Apprenticeship Council
500 C Street, NW, Suite 241
Washington, D.C. 20001

Delaware
Apprenticeship and Training
Section
Division of Employment &
Training
Delaware Department of Labor
USDL-BAT
Lock Box 36 - Federal Building
844 King Street
Wilmington, DE 19801
(302) 573-6113

Florida
USDL-BAT
City Centre Building, Suite 4140
227 North Bronaugh Street
Tallahassee, FL 32301
(904) 942-8336

Hawaii
Apprenticeship Division
USDL-BAT
Room 5113
300 Ala Moana Blvd.
Honolulu, HI 96850
(808) 541-2519

Kansas
USDL-BAT
444 SE Quincy St. - Room 247
Topeka, KS 66683-3571
(913) 295-2624

Kentucky
USDL-BAT
Federal Building - Room 187J
600 Martin Luther King Place
Louisville, KY 40202
(502) 582-5223

Louisiana
USDL-BAT
Suite 1043
501 Magazine Street
New Orleans, LA 70130
(504) 589-6103

Michigan
Apprenticeship Training
Division
USDL-BAT
801 S. Waverly - Room 304
Lansing, MI 48917
(517) 377-1746

Maine
USDL-BAT
Federal Building
68 Sewall Street - Room 401
Augusta, ME 04330
(207) 622-8235

Maryland
Apprenticeship & Training
Council
USDL-BAT
300 West Pratt Street
Room 200
Baltimore, MD 21201
(410) 962-2676

Massachusetts
USDL-BAT
Room E370
JFK Federal Bldg.
Boston, MA 02203
(617) 565-2291

Minnesota
Division of Apprenticeship
Department of Labor &
Industries
USDL-BAT
316 Robert St. - Room 146
St. Paul, MN 55101
(612) 290-3951

Montana
USDL-BAT
Federal Office Building
301 South Park Ave.
Room 396 - Drawer #10055
Helena, MT 59626-0055
(406) 441-1076

Nevada
USDL-BAT
301 Stewart Ave. - Room 311
Las Vegas, NV 89101
(702) 388-6396

New Hampshire
USDL-BAT
143 North Main St. - Room 205
Concord, NH 03301
(603) 225-1444

New Mexico
USDL-BAT
505 Marquette - Room 830
Albuquerque, NM 87102
(505) 766-2398

New York
USDL-BAT
Leo O'Brien Federal Building
Room 809
North Pearl & Clinton Avenue
Albany, NY 12207
(518) 431-4008

North Carolina
USDL-BAT
Somerset Park - Suite 205
4407 Bland Road
Raleigh, NC 27609
(919) 790-2801

Ohio
Ohio State Apprenticeship
USDL-BAT
Room 605
200 North High Street
Columbus, OH 43215
(614) 469-7375

Oregon
Apprenticeship & Training
USDL-BAT
Federal Building - Room 629
1220 SW 3rd Avenue
Portland, OR 97204
(503) 326-3157

Pennsylvania
USDL-BAT
Federal Building
228 Walnut Street - Room 773
Harrisburg, PA 17108
(717) 782-3496

Rhode Island
USDL-BAT
Federal Building
100 Hartford Avenue
Providence, RI 02909
(401) 528-5198

Vermont
USDL-BAT
Federal Building
11 Elmwood Ave. - Room 629
Burlington, VT 05401
(802) 951-6278

Virgin Islands
Division of Apprenticeship &
Training
Department of Labor
P.O. Box 890 Christiansted
St. Croix, Virgin Islands 00802

Virginia
USDL-BAT
700 Centre - Suite 546
704 East Franklin Street
Richmond, VA 23219
(804) 771-2488

Washington
USDL-BAT
Suite 100
1400 Talbot Road South
Renton, WA 98053
(206) 277-5214

Wisconsin
USDL-BAT
Federal Center - Room 303
212 East Washington Ave.
Madison, WI 53703
(608) 264-5377

**Oak Brook College of Law
and Public Policy**
P.O. Box 26870
Fresno, CA 93729
Phone (209) 261-9714
FAX (209) 261-9715
E-mail: obcl@aol.com
http://www.obcl.edu

Advanced Training Institute
Box 1
Oakbrook, IL 60522-3001
(630) 323-9800

Appendix B:
Home School Organizations

Alabama

Christian Home Education Fellowship of Alabama, P.O. Box 563, Alabaster, AL 35007; (205) 664-2232

Alaska

Alaska Private & Home Educators Association, P.O. Box 141764, Anchorage, AK 99514; (907) 696-0641

Arizona

Arizona Families for Home Education, P.O. Box 4661, Scottsdale, AZ 85261-4661; (602) 443-0612

Christian Home Educators of Arizona, P.O. Box 13445, Scottsdale, AZ 85267-3445

Flagstaff Home Educators, 6910 West Suzette Lane, Flagstaff, AZ 86001-8220; (520) 774-0806

Arkansas

Arkansas Christian Home Education Association, Box 4025, North Little Rock, AR 71290; (501) 758-9099

California

Christian Home Educators Association, P.O. Box 2009, Norwalk, CA 90651; (562) 864-2432 or (800) 564-CHEA

Family Protection Ministries, 910 Sunrise Avenue Suite A-1, Roseville, CA 95661

Colorado

Christian Home Educators of Colorado, 3739 E. 4th Avenue, Denver, CO 80206; (303) 388-1888

Concerned Parents for Colorado, P.O. Box 547, Florissant, CO 80902

Connecticut

The Education Association of Christian Homeschoolers, 25 Fieldstone Run, Farmington, CT 06032; (800) 205-7844 or (860) 667-4538

Delaware

Delaware Home Education Association, 1712 Marsh Road, Suite 172, Wilmington, DE 19810; (302) 475-0574

Tri-State Home School Network, 1712 Marsh Road, Suite 172, Wilmington, DE 19810-461; (302) 475-0574

District of Columbia

Bolling Area Home Schoolers of D.C., 1516-E Carswell Circle, Washington, DC 20336

Florida

Florida Parent-Educators Association, 3781 SW 18th Street, Ft. Lauderdale, FL 33312; (407) 723-1714

Florida Coalition of Christian Private School Administrators, 5813 Papaya Dr., Ft. Pierce, FL 34982; (407) 465-1685

Georgia

Georgia Home Education Association, 245 Buckeye Lane, Fayetteville, GA 30214; (770) 461-3657

North Georgia Home Education Association, 200 West Crest Road, Rossville, GA 30741

Hawaii

Christian Homeschoolers of Hawaii, 91-824 Oama Street, Ewa Beach, HI 96706; (808) 689-6398

Idaho

Idaho Home Educators, P.O. Box 1324, Meridian, ID 83680; (208) 323-0230

Illinois

Illinois Christian Home Educators, Box 310, Mt. Prospect, IL 60056; (847) 670-7150

Christian Home Educators Coalition, P.O. Box 470322, Chicago, IL 60647; (312) 278-0673

Indiana

Indiana Association of Home Educators, 850 North Madison Avenue, Greenwood, IN 46142; (317) 859-1202

Iowa

Network of Iowa Christian Home Educators, Box 158, Dexter, IA 50070; (515) 830-1614 or (800) 723-0438

Kansas

Christian Home Education Confederation of Kansas, P.O. Box 3564, Shawnee Mission, KS 66203; (913) 234-2927

Kentucky

Christian Home Educators of Kentucky, 691 Howardstown Road, Hodgensville, KY 42748; (502) 358-9270

Kentucky Home Education Association, P.O. Box 81, Winchester, KY 40392-0081; (606) 744-8562

Louisiana

Christian Home Educators Fellowship, P.O. Box 74292, Baton Rouge, LA 70874-4292; (504) 775-9709

Maine

Homeschoolers of Maine, HC62, Box 24, Hope, ME 04847; (207) 763-4251

Maryland

Maryland Association of Christian Home Educators, P.O. Box 247, Point of Rocks, MD 21777-0247; (301) 607-4284

Christian Home Educators Network, 304 North Beechwood Avenue, Catonsville, MD 21228; (410) 744-8919 or (410) 444-5465

Massachusetts

Massachusetts Homeschool Organization of Parent Educators, 5 Atwood Road, Cherry Valley, MA 01611-3332; (508) 755-4467

Michigan

Information Network for Christian Homes, 4934 Cannonsburg Road, Belmont, MI 49306; (616) 874-5656

Minnesota

Minnesota Association of Christian Home Educators, P.O. Box 32308, Fridley, MN 55432-0308; (612) 717-9070

Mississippi

Mississippi Home Educators Association, P.O. Box 945, Brookhaven, MS 39601; (601) 833-9110

Missouri

Missouri Association of Teaching Christian Homes, 307 East Ash Street, #146, Columbia, MO 65201; (573) 443-8217

Families for Home Education, 400 East High Point Lane, Columbia, MO 65203; (417) 782-8833

Montana

Montana Coalition of Home Educators, P.O. Box 43, Gallitin Gateway, MT 59730; (406) 587-6163

Nebraska

Nebraska Christian Home Educators Association, P.O. Box 57041, Lincoln, NE 68505-7041; (402) 423-4297

Nevada

Home Education And Righteous Training, P.O. Box 42262, Las Vegas, NV 89116; (702) 391-7219

Northern Nevada Home Schools, P.O. Box 21323, Reno, NV 89515; (702) 852-6647

New Hampshire

Christian Home Educators of New Hampshire, P.O. Box 961, Manchester, NH 03105; (603) 569-2343

New Jersey

Education Network of Christian Homeschoolers, 120 Mayfair Lane, Mount Laurel, NJ 08054; (609) 222-4283

New Mexico

Christian Association of Parent Educators of New Mexico, P.O. Box 25046, Albuquerque, NM 87125; (505) 898-8548

New York

Loving Education At Home, P.O. Box 88, Cato, NY 13033; (716) 346-0939

North Carolina

North Carolinians for Home Education, 419 N. Boylan Avenue, Raleigh, NC 27603; (919) 834-6243

North Dakota

North Dakota Home School Association, P.O. Box 7400, Bismarck, ND 58507-7400; (701) 223-4080

Ohio

Christian Home Educators of Ohio, 430 N. Court Street, Circleville, OH 43113; (614) 474-3177

Home Education Action Council of Ohio, P.O. Box 24133, Huber Heights, OH 45424; (513) 845-8428

Oklahoma

Christian Home Educators Fellowship of Oklahoma, P.O. Box 471363 Tulsa, OK 74147-1363; (918) 583-7323

Oklahoma Central Home Educators Consociation, P.O. Box 270601, Oklahoma City, OK 73137; (405) 521-8439

Oregon

Oregon Christian Home Education Association Network, 2515 N.E. 37th, Portland, OR 97212; (503) 288-1285

Pennsylvania

Christian Home School Association of Pennsylvania, P.O. Box 3603, York, PA 17402-0603; (717) 661-2428

Pennsylvania Homeschoolers, R.D. 2, Box 117, Kittanning, PA 16201; (412)783-6512

Rhode Island

Rhode Island Guild of Home Teachers, P.O. Box 11, Hope, RI 02831-0011; (401) 821-7700

South Carolina

South Carolina Home Educators Association, P.O. Box 612, Lexington, SC 29071; (803) 754-6425

South Carolina Association of Independent Home Schools, P.O. Box 2104, Irmo, SC 29063; (803) 551-1003

South Dakota

Western Dakota Christian Homeschools, P.O. Box 528, Black Hawk, SD 57118; (605) 923-1893

Tennessee

Tennessee Home Education Association, 3677 Richbriar Court, Nashville,TN 37211; (615) 834-3529

Texas

Home-Oriented Private Education for Texas, P.O. Box 59876, Dallas, TX 75229-9876; (214) 358-2221

Texas Home School Coalition, P.O. Box 6982, Lubbock, TX 79493; (806) 797-4927

North Texas Home Education Network, P.O. Box 59627, Dallas, TX 75229; (214) 234-2366

Family Educators Alliance of South Texas, 4719 Blanco Road, San Antonio, TX 78212; (210) 342-4674

South East Texas Home School Association, 4950 F.M. 1960W Suite C3-87, Houston, TX 77069; (713) 370-8787

Supporting Home Educators of Lower Texas Educational Region, 2424 Holden Road, Arkansas Pass, TX 78336; (512) 758-2777

Utah

Utah Christian Homeschoolers, P.O. Box 3942, Salt Lake City, UT 84110-3942; (801) 296-7198

Vermont

Christian Home Educators of Vermont, 214 N. Prospect #105, Burlington, VT 05401-1613; (802) 658-4561

Virginia

Home Educators Association of Virginia, P.O. Box 6745, Richmond, VA 23230-0745; (804) 288-1608

Washington

Washington Association of Teaching Christian Homes, N. 2904 Dora Road, Spokane, WA 99212; (509) 922-4811

Washington Homeschool Organization, 18130 Midvale Avenue North, Seattle, WA 98083

West Virginia

Christian Home Educators of West Virginia, P.O. Box 8770, South Charleston, WV 25303; (304) 776-4664

Wisconsin

Wisconsin Christian Home Educators, 2307 Carmel Avenue, Racine, WI 53405; (414) 637-5127

Wyoming

Homeschoolers of Wyoming, 339 Bicentennial Court, Powell, WY 82435; (307) 754-3271

Canada

Alberta Home Education Association, Box 3451, Leduc, Alberta, T9E 6M2; (403) 986-4264

England

Home Service, 48 Heaton Moor Road, Heaton Moor, Stockport SK4 4NX; 011-44-161-432-3782

Japan

KANTO Home Educators Association, PSC 477 Box 45, FPO, AP 96306-1299

Germany

Eifel Area Home Schoolers, 52 SPTG/MW, UNIT 3640 BOX 80, APO, AE 09126

Verna Lilly, PSC 118 Box 584, APO AE 09137; 011-49-6561-5341

New Zealand

Christian Home Schoolers of New Zealand, 4 Tawa Street, Palmerston North, New Zealand

Puerto Rico

Christian Home Educators of the Caribbean, Palmas Del Mar Mail Service, Box 888, Suite 273, Humacao, PR00791; (787) 852-5284

Handicapped

NATHHAN (National Challenged Homeschoolers Association Network), 5383 Alpine Road, S.E., Olalla, WA 98359; (206) 857-4257

Military

Christian Home Educators on Foreign Soil, Mike & Diane Smith, 1856 CSGP, PSC2 Box 8462, APO, AE 09012

Radio

Home Education Radio Network, P.O. Box 3338, Idaho Springs, CO 80452; (303) 567-4092

Appendix C:
Home School Laws of the United States

This analysis does not constitute the giving of legal advice. By definition, legislation is subject to frequent change. This analysis was current as of press time. For most up-to-date information, contact the Home School Legal Defense Association at 540-338-5600 or visit their web site at http://www.hslda.org.

State or Territory	Compulsory School Age	Legal Options to Home School	Attendance Requirements	Subjects Required
Alabama	"between the ages of 7 and 16"	Establish and/or enroll in a church school	180 days per year	Reading, spelling, writing, arithmetic, English, geography, history of the United States, science, health, physical education, and Alabama history
		Use a private tutor	140 days per year, 3 hours per day between the hours of 8 am and 4 pm	Reading, spelling, writing, arithmetic, English, geography, history of the United States, science, health, physical education, and Alabama history
Alaska	"between 7 and 16"	Use a private tutor	180 days per year	Comparable to those offered in the public schools
		Enroll in a state department of education approved full-time correspondence program	180 days per year	Comparable to those offered in the public schools

Teacher Qualifications	Notice Required	Recordkeeping Required	Testing Required
None	File a notice of enrollment and attendance with the local superintendent on a provided form (not required annually)	Maintain a daily attendance register	None
Teacher certification	File a statement showing children to be instructed, the subjects taught and the period of instruction with the local superintendent	Maintain a register of the child's work	None
Teacher certification	None	None	None
None	None	None	None

State or Territory	Compulsory School Age	Legal Options to Home School	Attendance Requirements	Subjects Required
Alaska (cont'd)	"between 7 and 16"	Request school board approval to provide an equal alternate educational experience	180 days per year	Comparable to those offered in the public schools
		Qualify as a religious or other private school	180 days per year	None, but standardized testing must cover English grammar, reading, spelling, and math
American Samoa	"between 6 and 18 years of age inclusive, or from grade one through grade twelve"	Request department of education authorization to operate a private school	Same as the public schools	A curriculum that is approved as being "in the interest of good citizenship" by the director of education
Arizona	"between 6 and 16"; however, a child under 8 on September 1 can be exempted upon written notice from the parent	Establish and operate a home school	None	Reading, grammar, math, social studies, and science

Teacher Qualifications	Notice Required	Recordkeeping Required	Testing Required
None	None	None	None
None	File a "Private School Enrollment Reporting Form" with the local superintendent by the first day of public school; also file a "Private and Denominational Schools Enrollment Report" and a "School Calendar" with the state department of education by October 15 each year	Maintain monthly attendance records; also maintain records on immunization, courses, standardized testing, academic achievement, and physical exams	Administer a standardized test in grades 4, 6, and 8
Teacher certification	A de facto part of the authorization process	Maintain permanent report cards; submit monthly enrollment reports and an annual report to the department of education	None
None	File an affidavit with the local superintendent within 30 days after home schooling begins or ends	None	None

State or Territory	Compulsory School Age	Legal Options to Home School	Attendance Requirements	Subjects Required
Arkansas	"5 through 17 on October 1 of that year, both inclusive"; a child that is under 6 by October 1 may be waived with submission of a state-provided form	Establish and operate a home school	None	None
California	"between the ages of 6" by December 2 and "under 18 years of age"	Qualify as a private school	None	Same as the public schools and in the English language
		Use a private tutor	175 days per year, 3 hours per day	Same as the public schools and in the English language
		Enroll in an independent study program through the public school	As prescribed by the program	As prescribed by the program
		Enroll in a private school satellite program, taking "independent study"	As prescribed by the program	As prescribed by the program

Teacher Qualifications	Notice Required	Recordkeeping Required	Testing Required
None	File written notice of intent with the local superintendent at beginning of each school year or when parent withdraws child from public school	None	Participate in same state-mandated norm-referenced tests given to public school students (in grades 5, 7, and 10); no cost to parent unless alternate testing procedures are approved
Must be "capable of teaching"	File an annual affidavit with the local superintendent between October 1 and 15	Maintain an attendance register	None
Teacher certification	None	None	None
None	A de facto part of the enrollment process	As prescribed by the program	As prescribed by the program
Must be "capable of teaching"	None	As prescribed by the program	As prescribed by the program

State or Territory	Compulsory School Age	Legal Options to Home School	Attendance Requirements	Subjects Required
Colorado	"7 and under the age of 16." Also "appl[ies] to a six-year-old child who has been enrolled in a public school in the first [or higher] grade," unless the "parent or legal guardian chooses to withdraw such a child"	Establish and operate a home school	172 days per year, averaging four hours per day	Constitution of the United States, reading, writing, speaking, math, history, civics, literature, and science
		Enroll in a private school that allows home instruction	None	As prescribed by the program
		Use a private tutor	None	Constitution of the United States, reading, writing, speaking, math, history, civics, literature, and science
Connecticut	"7 and under 16"	Establish and operate a home school	Generally, 180 days per year	Reading, writing, spelling, English, grammar, geography, arithmetic, United States history, and citizenship, including a study of the town, state, and federal governments

Teacher Qualifications	Notice Required	Recordkeeping Required	Testing Required
None	File notice of intent with the local superintendent 14 days prior to start of home school and annually thereafter	Maintain attendance records, test and evaluation results, and immunization records	Administer a standardized test for grades 3, 5, 7, 9, and 11 or have the child evaluated by a "qualified person… selected by parent"
None	None	None	None
Teacher certification	None	None	None
None	File a "Notice of Intent" form with the local superintendent within 10 days of the start of home school	Maintain a portfolio indicating that instruction in the required courses has been given	None

State or Territory	Compulsory School Age	Legal Options to Home School	Attendance Requirements	Subjects Required
Delaware	"between 5 years of age and 16 years of age"; can delay start (if "in best interests of the child") with school authorization	Establish and operate a home school providing "regular and thorough instruction" to the satisfaction of the local superintendent and the state board of education	180 days per year	Same as the public schools
		Establish and/or enroll in a private school	180 days per year	Same as the public schools
District of Columbia	"age of 5 years by December 31 of current school year until minor reaches the age of 18"	Provide private instruction not affiliated with an educational institution	During the period that the public schools are in session	None

Teacher Qualifications	Notice Required	Recordkeeping Required	Testing Required
None	None	None	Administer a written examination as prescribed during the approval process
None	School must submit an annual statement of enrollment before July 31 and another as of the last day of school in September, both to the state board of education	None	None
None	"Report to the Board the name, address, sex, and date of birth of each minor… who enrolls or withdraws from… school"	Maintain a daily attendance register	None

State or Territory	Compulsory School Age	Legal Options to Home School	Attendance Requirements	Subjects Required
Florida	"attained the age of 6 years by February 1 . . . but have not attained the age of 16 years"	Establish and operate a home school	Same as the public schools; generally, 180 days per year	English, math, science, history, government, physical education, fine arts
		Qualify and operate as part of a private school corporation (a legally incorporated group of home school families)	Same as the public schools; generally, 180 days per year	English, math, science, history, government, physical education, fine arts
Georgia	"between 7th and 16th birthdays"; a child under 7 who has attended public school for more than 20 days is also subject to the compulsory attendance law	Establish and conduct a home study program	180 days per year, 4 1/2 hours per day	Reading, language arts, math, social studies, and science

Teacher Qualifications	Notice Required	Recordkeeping Required	Testing Required
None	File notice of intent with the local superintendent within 30 days of establishment for home school (not required annually)	Maintain a portfolio of records and materials (log of texts and sample work sheets)	Annually, either: 1) administer any standardized test used by school district; must be given by a certified teacher, or 2) administer a state student assessment test, or 3) have child evaluated by a certified teacher, or 4) have child evaluated by another valid tool that is mutually agreed upon
None	None	None	None
High school diploma or GED for a teaching parent; baccalaureate degree for any private tutor used	File a declaration of intent with the local superintendent within 30 days of commencing the home study program and by September 1 annually thereafter	Maintain attendance records and submit monthly to the superintendent; write and retain an annual progress report	Administer and retain the results of a standardized test every 3 years beginning at the end of the 3rd grade

State or Territory	Compulsory School Age	Legal Options to Home School	Attendance Requirements	Subjects Required
Guam	"between the ages of 5 and 16 years"	Provide private instruction "by a private tutor or other person"	170 days per year	Same as the public schools and in the English language
Hawaii	"have arrived at the age of at least 6 years and... not... at the age of 18 years" by January 1	Establish and operate a home school	Same as the public schools	Curriculum must "be structured and based on educational objectives as well as the needs of the child, be cumulative and sequential, provide a range of up-to-date knowledge and needed skills, and take into account the interests, needs, and abilities of the child"
		Enroll in a superintendent-approved appropriate alternative educational program	As prescribed during the approval process (approximately 3 hours per day)	As prescribed during the approval process
Idaho	"attained the age of 7 years, but not the age of 16 years"	Provide an alternate educational experience for the child that "is otherwise comparably instructed"	Same as the public schools	Same as the public schools

Teacher Qualifications	Notice Required	Recordkeeping Required	Testing Required
None	None	None	None
None	File a notice of intent with the principal of the public school the child would otherwise be required to attend before starting to home school; notify this same principal within 5 days after ending home school	Maintain a record of the planned curriculum	Administer a standardized achievement test of parent's choice in grades 3, 6, 8, and 10
Baccalaureate degree	None	None	Participate in statewide testing program at the public schools
None	None	None	None

State or Territory	Compulsory School Age	Legal Options to Home School	Attendance Requirements	Subjects Required
Illinois	"between the ages of 7 and 16 years"	Operate a home school as a private school	Generally, 176 days per year (but not mandated for private or home schools)	Language arts, biological and physical science, math, social sciences, fine arts, health and physical development, honesty, justice, kindness, and moral courage
Indiana	"Earlier of the date on which the child officially enrolls in a school or reaches the age of 7 until the date on which he reaches the age of 17 or reaches the age of 16 and a parent or guardian provides written consent for the child to withdraw from school"	Operate a home school as a private school	Same as the public schools; generally, 180 days per year	None
Iowa	"age 6 by September 15 until age 16"	Establish and operate a home school	148 days per year (37 days each quarter)	None

Teacher Qualifications	Notice Required	Recordkeeping Required	Testing Required
None	None	None	None
None	None, unless specifically requested by the state superintendent of education	Maintain attendance records	None
None	Complete an annual "Competent Private Instruction Report Form"; file 2 copies with the local school district by 1st day of school or within 14 days of withdrawal from school	None	Complete by May 1 and submit to the local school district by June 30: 1) test results from an acceptably administered standardized test, or 2) a portfolio for review

State or Territory	Compulsory School Age	Legal Options to Home School	Attendance Requirements	Subjects Required
Iowa (cont'd)	"age 6 by September 15 until age 16"	Establish and operate a home school that is supervised by a licensed teacher	148 days per year (37 days each quarter)	None
		Use a private tutor	148 days per year (37 days each quarter)	None
Kansas	"reached the age of 7 and under the age of 18 years"	Operate a home school as a non-accredited private school	"substantially equivalent to...the public schools" (i.e., 186 days per year or 1116 hours per year; 1086 hours for 12th grade)	Reading, writing, arithmetic, geography, spelling, English grammar and composition, civil government, United States and Kansas history, patriotism and duties of a citizen, health, and hygiene
		Operate a home school as a satellite of an accredited private school	As prescribed by the supervising private school	As prescribed by the supervising private school

Teacher Qualifications	Notice Required	Recordkeeping Required	Testing Required
None for teaching parent; license for the supervising teacher	Complete an annual "Competent Private Instruction Report Form"; file 2 copies with the local school district by 1st day of school or within 14 days of withdrawal from school	None	None; however, must meet with supervising teacher twice per quarter (one may be conducted by telephone)
Teaching license	Complete an annual "Competent Private Instruction Report Form"; file 2 copies with the local school district by 1st day of school or within 14 days of withdrawal from school	None	None
Must be a "competent" teacher (however, local school board has no authority to define or evaluate "competence" of private school teachers)	Register name and address of school with the state board of education (not subject to approval)	None	None
Must be a "competent" teacher (however, local school board has no authority to define or evaluate "competence" of private school teachers)	None	As prescribed by the supervising private school	As prescribed by the supervising private school

State or Territory	Compulsory School Age	Legal Options to Home School	Attendance Requirements	Subjects Required
Kansas (cont'd)	"reached the age of 7 and under the age of 18 years"	Qualify for a state board of education approved religious exemption in the high school grades	As prescribed during the approval process	As prescribed during the approval process
Kentucky	"has reached the 6th birthday and has not passed the 16th birthday"	Qualify a home school as a private school	185 days per year	Reading, writing, spelling, math, and library research
Louisiana	"from the child's 7th birthday until his 17th birthday"	Establish and operate a home school as approved by the board of education	180 days per year	At least equal to the quality of that in the public schools including the Declaration of Independence and the Federalist Papers
		Operate a home school as a private school	180 days per year	At least equal to the quality of that in the public schools including the Declaration of Independence and the Federalist Papers

Teacher Qualifications	Notice Required	Recordkeeping Required	Testing Required
As prescribed during the approval process	A de facto part of the approval process	As prescribed during the approval process	As prescribed during the approval process
None	Notify the local board of education of those students in attendance within two weeks of start of school year	Maintain an attendance register and scholarship reports	None
None	File an application and a copy of the child's birth certificate, with board of education, within 15 days after start of home school and annually thereafter	Whatever form(s) of documentation is (are) planned to satisfy the testing requirement	Submit with renewal application documents showing satisfactory evidence that the program is at least equal to that offered by the public schools
None	Submit notification to the state department of education within the first 30 days of the school year	None	None

State or Territory	Compulsory School Age	Legal Options to Home School	Attendance Requirements	Subjects Required
Maine	"7 years of age or older and under 17 years"	Establish and operate a home school as approved by the local school board and the commissioner of the state department of education	175 days per year	English, language arts, math, science, social studies, physical and health education, library skills, fine arts, Maine studies (in one grade between grade 6 and 12), and computer proficiency (in one grade between grade 7 and 12)
		Operate a home school as a non-approved private school that teaches at least two unrelated students	175 days per year	None
Maryland	"5 years old or older and under 16" with one-year exemption available for 5-year-olds	Establish and operate a qualified home school	Must be of "sufficient duration to implement the instructional program"	Must provide "regular, thorough instruction" in the same subjects as the public schools including English, math, science, social studies, art, music, health, and physical education

Teacher Qualifications	Notice Required	Recordkeeping Required	Testing Required
None	Complete a state-provided "Application for Equivalent Instruction Through Home Instruction" form; submit a copy to both the local school board and the commissioner of the state department of education 60 days prior to start of home school	None	Annually, either: 1) administer a standardized test, or 2) take a local test, or 3) have child's progress reviewed by a certified teacher, a superintendent-selected local advisory board, or a home school support group that includes a certified teacher
None	None	None	None
None	File a notice of intent with the state department of education within 15 days of start of home school	Maintain a portfolio of "relevant materials," reviewable by the local superintendent up to 3 times per year	None

State or Territory	Compulsory School Age	Legal Options to Home School	Attendance Requirements	Subjects Required
Maryland (cont'd)	"5 years old or older and under 16" with one-year exemption available for 5-year-olds	Provide supervised home instruction through a church school or a state-approved correspondence course	As prescribed by the supervising program	As prescribed by the supervising program
Massachusetts	"6 to 16 years of age"	Establish and operate a home school as approved in advance by the local school committee or superintendent	None specified, though 900 hours at elementary level and 990 hours at secondary level are expected	Reading, writing, English language and grammar, geography, arithmetic, drawing, music, history, and constitution of United States, duties of citizenship, health (including CPR), physical education, and good behavior
Michigan	"age of 6 to the child's 16th birthday"	Establish and operate a home education program	None	Reading, spelling, mathematics, science, history, civics, literature, writing, and English grammar
		Operate a home school as a nonpublic school	None	Must be "comparable to those taught in the public schools"

Teacher Qualifications	Notice Required	Recordkeeping Required	Testing Required
None	File a notice of intent with the state department of education within 15 days of start of home school	As prescribed by the supervising program	As prescribed by the supervising program
None	A de facto part of the approval process	None	Annually, either: 1) administer a standardized test; must be administered by a neutral party, or 2) submit progress reports to the school district
None	None	None	None
Teacher certification (unless claiming a religious exemption)	Submit, to the local superintendent, at start of each school year a statement of enrollment	Maintain records of enrollment, courses of study, and qualifications of teachers (must be submitted to the Department of Education upon request)	None

State or Territory	Compulsory School Age	Legal Options to Home School	Attendance Requirements	Subjects Required
Minnesota	"between 7 and 16 years of age"; extends to 18 years old in the year 2000	Establish and operate a qualified home school	None	Reading, writing, literature, fine arts, math, science, history, geography, government, health, and physical education
Mississippi	"age of 6 on or before September 1... and has not attained the age of 17 on or before September 1"	Establish and operate a home school	Whatever "number of days that each [home] school shall require for promotion from grade to grade"	None
Missouri	"between the ages of 7 and 16 years"	Establish and operate a home school	1,000 hours per year; at least 600 hours in the five required subjects; 400 of these 600 hours must occur at "the regular home school location"	Reading, math, social studies, language arts, and science
		Operate a home school as a private school	None	None

Teacher Qualifications	Notice Required	Recordkeeping Required	Testing Required
None	File with the local superintendent by October 1 of each school year the name, age, and address of each child taught	If teaching parent is not at least a college graduate, submit a quarterly report to the local superintendent showing the achievement of each child in the required subjects	Administer an annual standardized test as agreed to by the local superintendent
None	File a "certificate of enrollment" by September 15 of each school year to the district's attendance officer	None	None
None	None required; parents "*may* provide" a notice of intent within 30 days of establish-ment and on September 1 each year thereafter	Maintain records of subjects taught, activities engaged in, samples of the child's academic work, and evalua-tions or a credible equivalent	None
None	None	None	None

State or Territory	Compulsory School Age	Legal Options to Home School	Attendance Requirements	Subjects Required
Montana	"7 years of age or older prior to the first day of school" and "the later of the following dates: the child's 16th birthday; the day of completion of the work of the 8th grade"	Establish and operate a home school	180 days per year, 4 hours per day for grades 1-3 and 6 hours per day for grades 4-12	Same "basic instructional program" as the public schools
Nebraska	"not less than 7 nor more than 16 years of age"	Establish and operate a home school as a private school	1,032 hours per year for elementary grades, 1,080 hours per year for high school grades	Language arts, math, science, social studies, and health
Nevada	"between the ages of 7 and 17 years"	Establish and operate a home school	180 days per year; 240 minutes per day for grades 1 and 2; 300 minutes per day for grades 3-6; 330 minutes per day for grades 7-12	Parents must provide the local school board with "satisfactory written evidence" that "the child is receiving at home ... equivalent instruction of the kind and amount approved by the state board of education," including U.S. and Nevada constitutions

Teacher Qualifications	Notice Required	Recordkeeping Required	Testing Required
None	File annual notice of intent with the local superintendent	Maintain attendance and immunization records; must be available for inspection by local superintendent upon request	None
None, unless the teacher is "employed" by the family	File a annual notice of intent with the state commissioner of education by August 1 (or 30 days prior to the start of home school)	None	None
Either: 1) possess a teaching certificate for the grade level taught, or 2) consult with a licensed teacher or 3-year home school veteran (waivable after 1st year), or 3) use an approved correspondence course, or 4) use a certified tutor	File, with the local school board, an annual request to have the child excused from compulsory attendance	None	Participate in the district-selected and administered standardized tests in grades 2 through 8 (unless a correspondence student); in grades 9-12, submit some form of documentation of progress (work samples, standardized test scores, etc.) as approved by the local school board

State or Territory	Compulsory School Age	Legal Options to Home School	Attendance Requirements	Subjects Required
New Hampshire	"at least 6 years of age [on September 30] and under 16 years of age"	Establish and operate a home school	None	Science, mathematics, language, government, history, health, reading, writing, spelling, U.S. and New Hampshire constitutional history, and art and music appreciation
New Jersey	"between the ages of six and 16 years"	Establish and operate a home school	Same as the public schools, not less than 180 days per year	U.S. and New Jersey history, citizenship, civics, geography, sexual assault prevention*, health*, safety, and physical education *may opt out*
New Mexico	"at least five years of age prior to 12:01 am on September 1 of the school year... to the age of majority... unless the person has graduated from high school"; children under eight can be excused	Establish and operate a home school	Same as the public schools	Reading, language arts, mathematics, social studies, and science

Teacher Qualifications	Notice Required	Recordkeeping Required	Testing Required
None	Within 30 days of withdrawing from public school or moving into the school district, file a notice of intent with a private school principal, the state commissioner of education, or the local superintendent	Maintain a portfolio of records and materials including a log of reading materials used, samples of writings, worksheets, workbooks or creative materials used or developed by the child	By July 1, file either: 1) results from a standardized test, or 2) results from a state student assessment test used by the local school district, or 3) a written evaluation by a certified teacher, or 4) results of another measure agreeable to the local school board
None	None	None	None
High school diploma or equivalent	File notice of intent with the school district superintendent within 30 days of establishing the home school and by April 1 of each subsequent year	Maintain attendance and immunization records	In grades 3, 5, & 8 either: 1) take the district-administered state achievement test, or 2) participate in the Bob Jones University Press Testing Service (*must notify the school board of intent by January 15*)

State or Territory	Compulsory School Age	Legal Options to Home School	Attendance Requirements	Subjects Required
New York	"a minor who becomes six years of age on or before the first of December in any school year... until the last day of session in the school year in which the minor becomes sixteen years of age" or completes high school	Establish and operate a home school	Substantial equivalent of 180 days per year; 900 hours per year for grades 1-6; 990 hours per year for grades 7-12	*Grades K-12*: patriotism and citizenship, substance abuse, traffic safety, fire safety; *Grades 1-6*: arithmetic, reading, spelling, writing, English, geography, U.S. history, science, health, music, visual arts, and physical education; *Grades 7-8*: English, history and geography, science, mathematics, physical education, health, art, music, practical arts, and library skills; *At least once in grades 1-8*: U.S. and New York history and constitutions; *Grades 9-12*: English, social studies—including American history, participation in government, and economics, math, science, art or music, health, physical education, and electives

Teacher Qualifications	Notice Required	Recordkeeping Required	Testing Required
"Competent"	File annual notice of intent with the local superintendent by July 1 or within 14 days if starting home schooling mid-year; complete and submit an Individualized Home Instruction Plan (form provided by district)	Maintain attendance records (must make available for inspection upon request of the local superintendent); file, with the local superintendent, quarterly reports listing hours completed, material covered, and a grade or evaluation in each subject	File, with the local superintendent, an annual assessment by June 30; must be from a standardized test every other year in grades 4-8, and every year in grades 9-12; other years can be satisfied by either another standardized test or a written narrative evaluation prepared by a certified teacher, a home instruction peer review panel, or other person chosen by the parent with the consent of the superintendent

State or Territory	Compulsory School Age	Legal Options to Home School	Attendance Requirements	Subjects Required
North Carolina	"between the ages of seven and 16 years"	Establish and operate a home school	At least nine calendar months per year, excluding reasonable holidays and vacations	None, but annual standardized tests must cover English grammar, reading, spelling, and mathematics
North Dakota	"any educable child of an age of seven years to sixteen years"	Establish and operate a home school	175 days per year, four hours per day	*Elementary*: spelling, reading, writing, arithmetic, language, English grammar, geography, U.S. history, civil government, nature, elements of agriculture, physiology and hygiene, effects of alcohol, prevention of contagious diseases, U.S. Constitution; *High School level*: English, math, science, social studies, health and physical education, music, combination of business, economics, foreign language, industrial arts, or vocational education

Teacher Qualifications	Notice Required	Recordkeeping Required	Testing Required
High school diploma or GED	File notice of intent with the state department of education upon starting home school	Maintain attendance and immunization records	Administer an annual standardized test measuring achievement in English grammar, reading, spelling, and mathematics, the results of which must be available for inspection
Possess either: 1) a teaching certificate, or 2) a baccalaureate degree, or 3) a high school diploma or GED and be monitored by a certified teacher (*waived after two years with test scores at or above 50th percentile*)	File annual notice of intent with the local superintendent 14 days prior to the start of the home school or within 14 days of establishing residency inside the district	Maintain an annual record of courses and each child's academic progress assessments, including standardized achievement test results	Take a standardized achievement test in grades 3, 4, 6, 8 and 11; must be administered by a certified teacher; results must be provided to the local superintendent

State or Territory	Compulsory School Age	Legal Options to Home School	Attendance Requirements	Subjects Required
Northern Mariana Islands	"between the ages of six and sixteen"	Seek approval to operate a home school	180 days per year with at least "300 minutes of secular instruction daily"	Same as the public schools
		Seek approval to operate a home school as an chartered non-public school	180 days per year with at least "300 minutes of secular instruction daily"	As prescribed by the board in issuing a charter
Ohio	"between six and eighteen years of age"	Establish and operate a home school	900 hours per year	Language arts, geography, U.S. and Ohio history, government, math, health, physical education, fine arts, first aid and science
Oklahoma	"over age of five (5) years and under the age of eighteen (18) years"	Establish and operate a home school as an "other means of education" expressed in the state constitution	None	Reading, writing, math, science, citizenship, U.S. constitution, health, safety, physical education, conservation
Oregon	"between the ages of 7 and 18 years who have not completed the twelfth grade"	Establish and operate a home school	Same as the public schools	Same as the public schools including U.S. constitution and history and primarily in the English language

Teacher Qualifications	Notice Required	Recordkeeping Required	Testing Required
None	Submit a waiver application to the commissioner at least 60 days prior to start of school year	Submit to the commissioner monthly, quarterly, and annual reports on program progress	None
None	Submit to the board of education an application for a charter	As prescribed by the board in issuing a charter	None
High school diploma, GED, test scores showing high school equivalence, or work under a person with a baccalaureate degree until child's test scores show proficiency or parent earns diploma or GED	Submit an annual notice of intent to the local superintendent	None	Submit with renewal notification either: 1) standardized test scores, or 2) a written narrative showing satisfactory academic progress, or 3) an approved alternative assessment
None	None	None	None
None	File, with the local superintendent an annual notice of intent 10 days before the start of each school year	None	Administer an approved annual standardized test; submit results to the local superintendent by October 31

State or Territory	Compulsory School Age	Legal Options to Home School	Attendance Requirements	Subjects Required
Pennsylvania	From time the child enters school, "which shall not be later than the age of eight (8) years, until the age of seventeen (17) years"	Establish and operate a home education program	180 days per year or 900 hours at the elementary level or 990 hours at the secondary level	*Elementary level*: English spelling, reading, and writing, arithmetic, U.S. and Pennsylvania history, civics, health and physiology, physical education, music, art, geography, science, safety and fire prevention *Secondary level*: English language, literature, speech and composition, science, geography, civics, world, U.S., and Pennsylvania history, algebra and geometry, art, music, physical education, health, safety, and fire prevention
		Establish and/or operate a home school as an extension or satellite of a private school	180 days per year or 900 hours at the elementary level or 990 hours at the secondary level	As prescribed by the program

Teacher Qualifications	Notice Required	Recordkeeping Required	Testing Required
High school diploma or equivalent	File a notorized affidavit with the local superinten-dent prior to the start of home school and annually by August 1st thereafter	Maintain a portfolio of materials used, work done, stan-dardized test results in grades 3, 5, and 8, and a written evaluation com-pleted by June 30 of each year	Administer standardized tests in grades 3, 5, and 8; submit results as part of portfolio
None	School principal must file a notarized affidavit with the depart-ment of education	None	None

State or Territory	Compulsory School Age	Legal Options to Home School	Attendance Requirements	Subjects Required
Puerto Rico	"between six and eighteen years of age"	Establish and operate a home school as a non-governmental school	Same as the public schools	Same as the public schools
Rhode Island	"completed six (6) years of life on or before December 31 of any school year and not completed sixteen (16) years of life"	Establish and operate a home school as approved by the local school board	"Substantially equal" to that of the public schools	Reading, writing, geography, arithmetic, U.S. and Rhode Island history, principles of American government, English, health and physical education; U.S. and R.I. constitution in high school
South Carolina	"five years of age before September first until... seventeenth birthday or" graduation from high school; five-year-olds may be excused from kindergarten with submission of written notice to the school district	Establish and operate a home school as approved by the local school board	180 days per year, 4 1/2 hours per day	Reading, writing, math, science, and social studies; also composition and literature in grades 7-12

Teacher Qualifications	Notice Required	Recordkeeping Required	Testing Required
None	None	None	None
None	A de facto part of the approval process	Maintain an attendance register	As prescribed during the approval process; may require report cards
High school diploma or GED or a baccalaureate degree	None	Maintain evidence of regular instruction including a record of subjects taught, activities in which the student and parent engage, a portfolio of the child's work, and a record of academic evaluations, with a semiannual progress report	Participate in the annual statewide testing program and the Basic Skills Assessment Program

State or Territory	Compulsory School Age	Legal Options to Home School	Attendance Requirements	Subjects Required
South Carolina (cont'd)	"five years of age before September first until... seventeenth birthday or" graduation from high school; five-year-olds may be excused from kinder-garten with submission of written notice to the school district	Establish and operate a home school under the membership auspices of the South Carolina Association of Independent Home Schools (SCAIHS)	180 days per year	Reading, writing, math, science, and social studies; also composi-tion and literature in grades 7-12
		Establish and operate a home school under the membership auspices of an association for home schools with no fewer than fifty members	180 days per year	Reading, writing, math, science, and social studies; also composi-tion and literature in grades 7-12
South Dakota	"six years old by the first day of September and who has not exceeded the age of six-teen years"; children under age 7 can be excused	Establish and operate a home school	Similar to that of the public schools; gener-ally 175 days per year	Language arts and math

Teacher Qualifications	Notice Required	Recordkeeping Required	Testing Required
High school diploma or GED	None	None	None
High school diploma or GED	None	Maintain evidence of regular instruction including a record of subjects taught, activities in which the student and parent engage, and a portfolio of the child's work, with a semiannual progress report	None
None	Submit a notarized application to the local superinten-dent using the standard form provided by state department of education	None	Administer a standardized test to children in the same grade levels tested under the state test-ing program (grades 4, 8, and 11)

State or Territory	Compulsory School Age	Legal Options to Home School	Attendance Requirements	Subjects Required
Tennessee	"between the ages of seven (7) and seventeen (17) years, both inclusive"; also applicable to children under age 7 who have enrolled in any public, private, or parochial school for more than six weeks	Establish and operate a home school	180 days per year, 4 hours per day	For grades K-8: None For grades 9-12: English, mathematics, science, Social Studies, and wellness; also must take college preparation subjects according to declared path—foreign language and fine arts for University path; focus area for tech path
		Establish and operate a home school in association with a church-related school	As prescribed by the church-related school	As prescribed by the church-related school
Texas	"as much as six years of age, or who is less than seven years of age and has previously been enrolled in first grade, and who has not completed the academic year in which his 17th birthday occurred"	Establish and operate a home school as a private school	None	Reading, spelling, grammar, math, good citizenship

Teacher Qualifications	Notice Required	Recordkeeping Required	Testing Required
For grades K-8: High school diploma or GED *For grades 9-12*: College degree (or an exemption granted by the commissioner of education)	Submit a notice of intent to the local superintendent by August 1 of each school year	Maintain attendance records; must be kept available for inspection and submitted to the local superintendent at the end of the school year	Administer a standardized test in grades 2, 5, 7, and 9; must be given by commissioner of education, his designee, or a professional testing service approved by the local school district
For grades K-8: None *For grades 9-12*: High school diploma or GED	*For grades K-8*: None *For grades 9-12*: Register with the local school district each year	None	Administer the same annual standardized achievement test or Sanders Model assessment used by the local school district for grades 9-12
None	None	None	None

State or Territory	Compulsory School Age	Legal Options to Home School	Attendance Requirements	Subjects Required
Utah	"between six and 18 years of age"	Establish and operate a home school as approved by the local school board	Same as the public schools	Language arts, math, science, social studies, arts, health, computer literacy, and vocational education
		Establish a group of home school families as a regular private school	None	None
Vermont	"between the ages of seven and sixteen years"	Establish and operate a home school	175 days per year	Reading, writing, math, citizenship, history, U.S. and Vermont government, physical education, health, English, science, and fine arts
Virgin Islands	"beginning of the school year nearest [child's] fifth birthday... until the expiration of the school year nearest [child's] sixteenth birthday," except those who graduate from high school earlier	Seek commissioner of education approval to establish and operate a home school	As prescribed during the approval process	As prescribed during the approval process

Teacher Qualifications	Notice Required	Recordkeeping Required	Testing Required
None specified; however, the local school board can consider the basic educative ability of the teacher	A de facto part of the approval process	None	None
None	None	None	None
None	File a written notice of enroll-ment with the commissioner of education any time after March 1 for the subsequent year	None	Submit an annual assessment from: 1) a certified (or approved Vermont independent school) teacher, or 2) a report from a commercial curriculum publisher together with a port-folio, or 3) results of an acceptably administered stan-dardized test
As prescribed during the approval process	A de facto part of the approval process	As prescribed during the approval process	As prescribed during the approval process

State or Territory	Compulsory School Age	Legal Options to Home School	Attendance Requirements	Subjects Required
Virgin Islands (cont'd)	"beginning of the school year nearest [child's] fifth birthday... until the expiration of the school year nearest [child's] six-teenth birth-day," except those who graduate from high school earlier	Apply for accreditation to operate a home school as a private school	As prescribed during the accreditation process	As prescribed during the accreditation process
Virginia	"have reached the fifth birthday on or before... September 30... and who has not passed the eighteenth birthday; 5-year-olds can be excused	Establish and operate a home school	Same as the public schools; generally 180 days per year	Reading, writing, math, spelling, history, government and citizenship
		Operate a home school under the religious exemption statute	None	None
		Use a private tutor	None	None

Teacher Qualifications	Notice Required	Recordkeeping Required	Testing Required
As prescribed during the accreditation process	A de facto part of the accreditation process	As prescribed during the accreditation process	As prescribed during the accreditation process
Either: 1) possess a baccalaureate degree, or 2) be a certified teacher, or 3) use an approved correspondence course, or 4) submit acceptable curriculum and prove the parent can teach	File an annual notice of intent with local superintendent by August 31	None	Administer a standardized test or have child otherwise evaluated every year; submit results to local superintendent by August 1
None	Submit a notice of intent to local school board	None	None
Teacher certification	File an annual notice of intent with the local superintendent by August 31	None	None

State or Territory	Compulsory School Age	Legal Options to Home School	Attendance Requirements	Subjects Required
Washington	"eight years of age and under eighteen years of age"	Establish and operate a home school	*For grades 1-3*: at least 2,700 total hours; *For grades 4-6*: at least 2,970 total hours; *For grades 7-8*: at least 1,980 total hours; *For grades 9-12*: at least 4,320 total hours	Occupational education, science, math, language, social studies, history, health, reading, writing, spelling, music and art appreciation, U.S. and Washington constitutions
		Operate a home school as an extension of an approved private school	*For grades 1-3*: at least 2,700 total hours; *For grades 4-6*: at least 2,970 total hours; *For grades 7-8*: at least 1,980 total hours; *For grades 9-12*: at least 4,320 total hours	Occupational education, science, math, language, social studies, history, health, reading, writing, spelling, music and art appreciation, U.S. and Washington constitutions
West Virginia	"compulsory school attendance shall begin with the school year in which the sixth birthday is reached prior to the first day of September of such year or upon enrolling in a publicly supported kindergarten program and continue to the sixteenth birthday"	Seek local school board approval to operate a home school	Same as the public schools; generally 180 days per year	English, grammar, reading, social studies, and math

Teacher Qualifications	Notice Required	Recordkeeping Required	Testing Required
Either: 1) be supervised by a certified teacher, or 2) have 45 college quarter credit hours or completed a course in home education, or 3) be deemed qualified by the local superintendent	File an annual notice of intent with the local (or applicable nonresident) superintendent by September 15 or within two weeks of the start of any public school quarter	Maintain standardized test scores, academic progress assessments, and immunization records	Annually, administer and retain a state approved standardized test by a qualified person or have the child evaluated by a certified teacher
None	None	None	None
Be deemed qualified to teach by the local superintendent and school board	A de facto part of the approval process	As prescribed during the approval process	As prescribed during the approval process

State or Territory	Compulsory School Age	Legal Options to Home School	Attendance Requirements	Subjects Required
West Virginia (cont'd)	"compulsory school attendance shall begin with the school year in which the sixth birthday is reached prior to the first day of September of such year or upon enrolling in a publicly supported kindergarten program and continue to the sixteenth birthday"	Establish and operate a home school	None	English, grammar, reading, social studies, and math
Wisconsin	"between the ages of 6 [by September 1] and 18 years"	Establish and operate a "home-based private educational program"	Must provide "at least 875 hours of instruction each year"	Must provide "a sequentially progressive curriculum of fundamental instruction" in reading, language arts, math, social studies, science, and health; such curriculum need not "conflict with the program's religious doctrines"

Teacher Qualifications	Notice Required	Recordkeeping Required	Testing Required
High school diploma and formal education at least four years higher than the most academically advanced child to be taught	File a notice of intent with the local superintendent two weeks prior to starting to home school	None	Annually, either: 1) administer an acceptable standardized test, or 2) be evaluated by a certified teacher, or 3) assess progress by another agreeable means
None	File a statement of enrollment with the state department of education by October 15 each year	None	None

State or Territory	Compulsory School Age	Legal Options to Home School	Attendance Requirements	Subjects Required
Wyoming	"whose seventh birthday falls before September 15 of any year and who has not yet attained his sixteenth birthday or completed the eighth grade"	Establish and operate a home school	175 days per year	A "basic academic educational program" that provides a sequentially progressive curriculum of fundamental instruction in reading, writing, math, civics, history, literature, and science
		Operate a home school under the auspices or control of a local church, religious congregation, or denomination	None	None

Teacher Qualifications	Notice Required	Recordkeeping Required	Testing Required
None	Annually submit to the local school board a curriculum showing that a "basic academic educational program" is being provided	None	None
None	None	None	None

Index

Abortion, 38, 42, 45

Academic achievement: failures of public schools, 5–7; home school children compared to national average, xi, xii, xxxi, 4; income as a predictor of, xviii, xxii–xxiii

Academic counseling, 19, 51, 57, 65–67

ACLU. *See* American Civil Liberties Union

Acronyms, 60

Activism. *See* Politics of home schooling

Adams, John Quincy, 4, 22

Administrative assistance, 57, 65

Advanced Training Institute, 115

Advertising, 13

Age segregation, 85

Alabama: child abuse investigations, 39, 41

Alcohol use, 124

Allen, George, 44

American Civil Liberties Union, 41, 42

American Girl history program, 53

American studies: as part of classical education, 16, 19

Anonymous Tip, 38

Apprenticeship: benefits of, 24, 107; certification, 108; college and, 112–113; description, 107–108; Farris' experience with, 108–110; journeyman status, 108; materials, 122; model programs, 120–121; modern "masters," 117–118; opportunities for, 113–116; pastors, 118–120; publicizing successes, 121–122; Switzerland's programs, 111–112, 115; tax breaks for, 115